THE BOOK OF
Wizard Magic

In Which the Apprentice finds Marvelous Magic Tricks, Mystifying Illusions & Astonishing Tales

LARK BOOKS

A Division of Sterling Publishing Company, Inc.

NEW YORK

AUTHORS
Janice Eaton Kilby
Terry Taylor

ILLUSTRATION
Lindy Burnett

ART DIRECTOR
Susan McBride

ASSISTANT EDITORS
Veronika Alice Gunter
Rain Newcomb

ASSISTANT ART DIRECTOR
Hannes Charen

TECHNICAL ILLUSTRATION
Orrin Lundgren

Library of Congress Cataloging-in-Publication Data

10 9 8 7 6 5 4 3 2 1

First Edition

Published by Lark Books, a division of
Sterling Publishing Co., Inc.
387 Park Avenue South, New York, N.Y. 10016

© 2003, Lark Books

Distributed in Canada by Sterling Publishing,
c/o Canadian Manda Group, One Atlantic Ave., Suite 105
Toronto, Ontario, Canada M6K 3E7

Distributed in the U.K. by:
Guild of Master Craftsman Publications Ltd.
Castle Place
166 High Street
Lewes
East Sussex
England
BN7 1XU
Tel: (+ 44) 1273 477374
Fax: (+ 44) 1273 478606
Email: pubs@thegmcgroup.com
Web: www.gmcpublications.com

Distributed in Australia by Capricorn Link (Australia) Pty Ltd.,
P.O. Box 704, Windsor, NSW 2756 Australia

The written instructions, photographs, designs, patterns, and projects in this
volume are intended for the personal use of the reader and may be reproduced for
that purpose only. Any other use, especially commercial use, is forbidden under law
without written permission of the copyright holder.

Every effort has been made to ensure that all the information in this book is
accurate. However, due to differing conditions, tools, and individual skills, the
publisher cannot be responsible for any injuries, losses, and other damages that
may result from the use of the information in this book.

If you have questions or comments about this book, please contact:
Lark Books
67 Broadway
Asheville, NC 28801
(828) 253-0467

Printed in China

ISBN 1-57990-345-2

Acknowledgments

How is it possible that this is the
Wizard's third book? It must be
magic! Gratitude and thanks are due
to my astonishing fellow wizards
Terry Taylor, Susan McBride, Lindy
Burnett, Hannes Charen, Veronika
Gunter, and Rain Newcomb. Love
always to Tip, Ryan, and Angela
Kilby, where everything started. And
let us not forget Lady Tze, patroness
of female wizards and wordsmiths
everywhere.

JEK

Is it possible that this will be the
Wizard's final communiqué from the
Great Unknown? Only time will tell.

TBT

TABLE OF

CONTENTS

Chapter 1
ORIGINS of MAGIC

What's the first thing people think of when they think of wizards? Obviously, magical powers that are outside the realm of mere mortals. PRESTO! Appear and disappear. SHAZAAM! Change one thing into another. ALAKAZAAM! Make objects fly, defy gravity, or zip invisibly from one spot to another. So it's time you learned how to do this, young wizard—or to make people believe you can, which is almost the same thing.

By learning how to create fabulous illusions and to perform magic tricks, you'll join a long line of wizards, magicians, and conjurors who have fun amazing other people by doing the seemingly impossible. It's handy to have a few tricks and illusions up your sleeve while you're still learning to be a real wizard. (And they make a good backup if you're having an off day with your wizardly powers.) So I'm going to share what I've learned about magic with you, and since I'm 600 years old and a wizard myself, that's quite a lot.

Some of our best illusions are hundreds—even thousands—of years old, and they come from around the world. Legend says magic is the art of the Magi, the priests of ancient Persia. But the Persians actually learned what they knew from the Egyptians.

The Magic Arts of Ancient Egypt

If you can read hieroglyphics, there's a 4,000-year-old papyrus in a German museum that tells the story of Dedi, one of our earliest wizards. Remember Cheops, the pharaoh who built the Great Pyramid? One rainy afternoon, his sons told him stories of a wizard who changed a life-size, wax model of a crocodile into a real animal, then changed it back—after it ate someone. They also described Jajamanekh, another wizard who said a few magic words to stack half of a lake's water on top of itself so he could retrieve a lady's lost bauble! Boyish fantasies, thought His Royal Magnificence.

But one wizard still lived, insisted the young princes. Named Dedi, he was 110 years old and ate enough food to feed hundreds of people daily. Dedi could reattach heads to decapitated bodies, bringing them back to life, and lions followed him like tame temple cats! Dedi also knew the layout of the secret chambers at the temple of Thoth, the Egyptian god of magic. This got Cheops's attention, because he'd always wanted to copy Thoth's floor plans for his own tomb in the Great Pyramid. So the royal barge was sent up the Nile for Dedi.

In front of Cheops, the wizard reattached the severed heads of a goose, a pelican, and an ox, and the animals scampered away. (He declined Cheops' offer of a human.) And sure enough, a lion from the king's zoo padded after Dedi, its leash trailing on the floor, according to the papyrus, anyway.

I'm six centuries old, but this all happened long before my time, and I simply can't tell you if Dedi used real wizard's magic to make those things happen. Perhaps he secretly reached into his robe to substitute a live goose for the headless and very dead one. (Hmm. I'm not sure how he'd do that with an ox. It's a mystery.) In any event, I forbid you to climb into a cage with a lion or to cut the head off ANYTHING. We're more civilized these days, and this book will teach you plenty of other ways to amaze your family and friends with fantastic illusions from ancient times and faraway lands.

In addition to Egypt, India and China were chock-full of wizards and conjurers who kept busy vanishing up ropes that stretched into the sky (see page 119). Magicians learned their craft in schools in ancient Greece, and on the streets of Imperial Rome, you could see the trick we still know today as the Cups and Balls! Street magic travelled with the Roman Empire, and magicians performed jugglery, as it was called in England, for commoners in the street and royalty in their castles.

Some people feared conjurers because they thought their powers might really be supernatural. Well, between you and me, here's the big secret: They were right! We wizards like to get out and about as much as the next person. Plus, how else are we going to keep our powers sharp? We all practice in the privacy of our chambers, but it's fun to see what we can do in front of an audience.

Medieval Magic and Wizards in Every Village

In the old days, every village had a wizard or witch. Legend says that fairies taught them their magical secrets. Want to hear something funny? When those ridiculous hunts for "bad" witches began during the Middle Ages, it was actually good for business. Many people became so scared of evil magic, they went running to the good witch next door for protective charms and spells! Let that be a lesson to us all.

Magic became all the rage when Queen Elizabeth I ruled England in the 1500s, and performance magic was as popular as sports events and the theater. John Dee was the most famous magician of the era and one of the Queen's house wizards. But over the next couple of centuries, as science explained more of the workings of nature, people began to forget the powers we wizards have. If you can believe it, some of us had to go out and start earning a living as illusionists! By the mid-1700s, many of my friends were working as stage magicians, charging admission to their shows. (Sometimes they'd even flub a trick on purpose to reassure their audience that nothing too uncanny was happening.)

OF COURSE, WE WIZARDS ALSO SHARED SOME TRICKS WITH OUR NONWIZARD FRIENDS WHO WANTED TO MAKE MAGIC TOO. . .

Pinetti, the Roman Professor of Mathematics and Natural Philosophy

My charismatic Italian friend Giovanni Guiseppe Pinetti (Gigi to his friends) became very famous in the 1780s and 1790s. He once taught physics but realized there was more money in magic. Gigi liked to pretend his tricks were based on arcane scientific principles he'd discovered in his laboratory, but he really was restaging illusions used by earlier magic folk. (As the Greeks liked to say, there is nothing new under *Helios*.)

Gigi could take off a man's shirt without removing his coat, read people's thoughts, and shoot a nail through a card someone chose from a deck and pin it to the wall! (My Ultra-Accurate Velocity Charm worked wonders for his act, though he catapulted his poor cat through the window a few times until he got it right.) He packed Europe's best theaters and performed for royalty, including the King of France, the Russian Czar, and King George III.

MAGIC
in the New World

As missionaries, traders, and colonists arrived in the Americas, there were plenty of local wizards to greet them. When that smelly old Spanish mercenary Hernando Cortez was crashing around the South American jungle looking for gold, the locals did sleight-of-hand for him. French missionaries described Canada as "a nation of sorcerers" and wrote about the medicine men who threw bags which changed into snakes on the ground, and who made miniature clay Indians and buffaloes which came to life and chased each other around campfires!

In the British colonies, survival was a serious business. All hands were needed to raise food and defend against Indian attack, so magicians and conjurors were considered useless and were barred from performing! Hmpf. The Dutch in New York City were more tolerant, as were our sophisticated cousins in England and Europe.

Jacob Philadelphia and His Phantasms

In the late 1700s, my friend Jacob Philadelphia became the first American-born magician to tour Europe with great success, performing for Catherine the Great of Russia and the Sultan of Turkey. Jacob combined sleight of hand with the display of marvelous objects, such as a pen that wrote in several colors (People thought Jacob invented it. I didn't mind.) His masterpiece was the production of ghostly figures that shimmered and floated about on stage. Some people fled the theater in terror! My German friend, the writer Johann Wolfgang von Goethe, saw Jacob's performance. Like many writers, Johann knew a good idea when he saw one, and he later wrote *Faust*, his famous story about a 16th-century conjurer.

Richard Potter, an American Success Story

Richard Potter was the first American-born magician to become a success in his own country. Born in 1783 to a Boston tax collector and an African slave, he grew up to become a huge success as a ventriloquist, birdcall imitator, and performer of "100 Curious but Mysterious Experiments," including, and I am not kidding about this, a "Dissertation on Noses." Some people claimed that Richard drove a cart pulled by geese, he passed through solid tree trunks at will, and he had a magic rooster that could pull a loaded wagon. Personally, I think a wizard should be a bit more, well, discreet with his powers. But no harm came to Richard, and he became very wealthy indeed, living with his lovely Penobscot Indian wife and children in a huge mansion on a 200-acre farm.

9

SIGNOR ANTONIO BLITZ, Professor of Mechanism & Metamorphosis

During the nineteenth century, many European magicians started taking the boat to the Americas, where they saw lots of wizard gold to be made. Trained by Moravian gypsies (well, it sounded good in his ads), Antonio Blitz amused and astonished audiences with his 500 trained canaries. I have warm memories of my friend's kindness. When a little girl came backstage with her (quite dead) pet canary and asked him to revive it, Blitz gave her one of his own birds. One dark and stormy night in Philadelphia, the curtain opened and Blitz saw only two people in the theater. A mother and son had travelled a very long way to see him. Rather than disappoint, Blitz gave his full two-hour performance for his audience of two, who went home happy. Remember, true wizards are generous!

Queen Victoria Meets the Great Wizard of the North

Sometimes the best way to hide something is to put it in plain view. So why do you think the 19th-century Scottish magician John Henry Anderson billed himself as The Caledonian Conjuror, The Great Wizard of the North, and The Napoleon of Necromancy, hmm? During the time Victoria ruled England, there was also a Wizard of the West, a Royal Wizard of the South, and two more Wizards of the North performing on stage. I vividly remember the old Egyptian Hall in London, with its velvet curtains, sphinxes, and the odd mummy staggering about. Every stage wizard dreamed of performing there. The rest of us came to cheer them on.

European and British royalty were mad for magic like everyone else. The Queen summoned the Great Wizard to perform at the birthday of her son, the Prince of Wales. Anderson outdid himself, levitating his own son, releasing a cloud of doves from his Enchanted Cauldron, and serving drinks from his Inexhaustible Bottle. The Queen's favorite trick was Anderson's Magic Scrapbook. From a thin, empty portfolio, the Wizard produced hats, plates, a live goose, vases of flowers, bowls of goldfish, and finally, the little Prince of Wales himself!

Americans went wild when Anderson finally made it across the Atlantic. He even performed for Kamehameha IV, the King of Hawaii, giving the monarch a trick glove that shocked anyone who shook his hand. The king loved it and insisted on trying it out on all his courtiers. Presidents loved magic as much as royalty. Even at the height of the American Civil War, Abraham Lincoln took the time to watch magician Carl Hermann do card tricks at the White House. Lincoln's secretary of war even shuffled the pack of cards! Hermann was famous for his accuracy in throwing cards to all parts of an opera house or theater, but I doubt he threw any at the dignified American president.

Robert-Houdin &
Wizard Diplomacy

All kidding aside, heads of state used wizards—er, I mean magicians—for much more serious matters. In 1856, Emperor Napoleon III sent the famous French magician Robert-Houdin to Algeria to convince rebellious desert tribes to, well, stop rebelling. As symbols of French power, the magician produced cannon balls from hats and coins from a locked chest, then he made a young Moor disappear from beneath a cloth cone. The terrified audience stampeded from the theater! A few days later, the tribal leaders returned to demonstrate their continued loyalty to France.

THE QUEEN of Magic

What about our sister sorceresses and female illusionists? Impossible to forget flame-haired Adelaide of the world-famous Hermann family, which dominated the world of magic for more than 80 years. Adelaide had real spirit. She was among the first women to be fired from a cannon and to perform on an old-fashioned bicycle, the really tall kind with a huge front wheel. At age 75, the Queen of Magic was still on tour, producing hundreds of silk scarves from thin air and disappearing her assistants (she usually got them back). Newspapers claimed she'd found the fountain of youth, but between you and me, here's the real story. My alchemist friend Nicholas Flamel had seen Adelaide on stage in Paris, and he was so captivated, he gave her some of his Elixir of Life. (Don't tell Mrs. Flamel.)

Harry Kellar &
HOW to MAKE MAGIC
FROM (ALMOST) NOTHING

Big-time stage wizardry is wonderful,
but you can make magic from everyday objects too. My favorite example
of this is a story about the American
illusionist Harry Kellar. Once, one of
Harry's business partners skipped
town with all the money from
Harry's stage show. Harry was left
penniless, but he didn't give up! After
talking a printer into printing some
show posters on credit, Harry borrowed two packs of playing cards and
an opaque glass bottle from a friendly
saloonkeeper (for his trick of break-
ing open the bottle to find a ring), a
set of baby clothes (to come out of a
borrowed hat), and metal cups (to be
magically filled with coffee, milk, and
sugar). Harry was in business again,
and his next show sold out. Similarly,
when a theater fire destroyed the
scenery, equipment, and costumes of
Wiljalba Frikell (no, I did not make
up that name), the magician
appeared in street clothes on a bare
stage and did simple tricks with
everyday objects. The audience
loved it! YOU GET MY POINT.

Hopefully, my dear young wizard, these stories have given you a sense of magic's long, rich heritage. Give respect where it's due to stage wizards everywhere, but let's not take ourselves too seriously, either. The point is to have fun! So if you're ready to learn how to make magic, turn the page to get on with the show!

MAGICA MANUALIS

Hands-On Hints for Making Magic

I never met a young wizard or sorceress who
didn't want to perform newly learned magic
for friends and family. Here are some useful
tips I've learned from my magician friends
over the past several hundred years.

PRACTICE, Practice, Practice

Whether you make magic in front of
an audience of two or 20, you should
practice what you're going to do and
what you're going to say at every step
of the illusion. Work in front of a full-
length mirror so you can see what
your audience will see. (Make sure
they can't detect your hand reaching
into in a secret pocket,
for example.)

Practice your hand and body
movements until you move naturally,
fluidly, and without hesitation. When
the time comes to perform, slow
down! Don't speed through your
tricks so quickly that your audience
doesn't have time to absorb them.

Make your gestures large enough that
your audience can see what you're
doing, and be sure to hold props in
such a way that they can be seen too.
It's better to perform a small number
of tricks very well than a large number
badly. One of our most famous mortal
magicians, John Nevil Maskelyne,
admitted he was really good at only a
half-dozen illusions.

Misdirection

Misdirection is the key to successful
magic. The magician looks at, or calls
attention to, an object or action that
has nothing to do with producing the
magical effect. While the audience
members focus their attention there
too, they won't pay attention to the
place where the, ahem, real magic is

taking place (such as when you secretly pocket a ring). Don't tell your audience exactly what magical effect to
expect from a trick, or they'll be looking in places you don't want them to.

You need to become so comfort-
able with a piece of magic that you
can talk, do something with your
hands (sometimes different things
with different hands), and think ahead
to the next step of the performance all
at the same time.

Palming

Some illusions in this book depend
on using secret objects the audience
never sees. Other tricks, such as the
Disappearing Magic Ring (page 44),
depend on the sleight of hand technique called palming. That's when

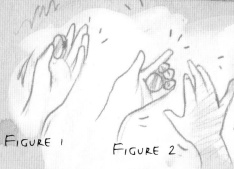

FIGURE 1   FIGURE 2

you hide a small object in the palm of your hand without letting viewers see what you're doing. You might start a trick with an object hidden in your hand, which you later produce. Or you might show the audience an object, then hide it in your hand while you lead them to think it has disappeared or travelled somewhere else.

In a move called the French Drop, a magician holds a coin or small object between the thumb and three fingers of the left hand (fig. 1). The magician covers the coin with the right hand, closes the fingers, and pretends to take away the coin. But he really loosens his left thumb's pressure on the coin so the coin drops to the base of the left fingers (fig. 2). So when the magician holds up his right hand and opens the fingers— gasp!—it has disappeared!

When you practice palming, study your hand movements in a mirror and try to make them look as normal as possible. If your hands still look slightly unnatural, you can misdirect your audience by making the same (unnatural) hand movements before you even do the trick. That way they won't notice anything out of the ordinary happening. And

never look at the hand that holds a palmed object or performs a secret movement, or your audience will too.

Patter

You must never have dead silence during a magic show. Either you should be talking, music should be playing, or the audience should be laughing or applauding. Practice what you'll say while you perform. That's called patter, and it links together the steps of an illusion and helps misdirect viewers' attention. For some illusions in this book, I've given you specific suggestions on what to say. Adapt the stories I tell or make up your own. I also share some handy commands and spells (see page 37) that you can use during your performance.

Setting the Stage for a Show

Decide ahead of time the best way to use your performance space, whether it's a basement or a stage. Plan exactly where you'll stand. Some illusions, such as the Mysterious Celestial Sphere (page 77), depend on using threads that should remain invisible to the audience. So put distance between you and your audience, and perform against a dark background (see the Stage Backdrop on page 22). Use dim lighting (red lightbulbs are even better), and position yourself

with the light at your back so your shadow falls over the thread.

Order your tricks for increasingly dramatic effects. (I've included a showstopper illusion in every chapter for a wham-bang finish!) Make a prop list of all the objects and materials needed for every trick. Lay them out in order in your performance area, perhaps on and around your Magician's Stage Table (page 19). Double check that everything's there just before the show.

R-E-S-P-E-C-T Your Audience

Happy audiences like to believe certain things. Number one, that you're a real wizard (so act like one). Number two, that everything is happening right then and there in real time and onstage (no need for them to know you had the help of a trusty assistant in Messages from the Ether on page 132).

And my third bit of advice: Never, ever tell how a trick is done, no matter how much they beg! Really. Trust me on this. It's considered very bad form in the magical world to divulge secrets to nonmagicians. And even though some people may suspect how you created an illusion, they're much happier believing that they're seeing real magic! Besides, you can probably produce the same effect by wizardly means once you've studied some more.

NOW GO MAKE SOME MAGIC!

Chapter 2

MAGICAL APPAREL & APPURTENANCES

To be a successful stage wizard, you must have the right tools and look the part. But good grief, don't go as far as the Greek sorceress Erichtho, who wore a necklace of live snakes! I find my All-Purpose Performance Robe to be very useful. (Secret pockets are the key, see page 32.) Add drama with a Cloak of Mystery (page 26), and craft a Never-Fail Magic Wand and a Thin Air Scarf to levitate and disappear all sorts of things (pages 18 and 35). If you decide to take your show on the road, you'll need a High-Mileage Magician's Travel Trunk (see my design on page 20). And don't forget to create a stage name for yourself. My good friend the novelist Charles Dickens was also a keen amateur magician. He called himself "The Unparalleled Necromancer, Rhia Rhama Rhoos." Charlie never used one word where three would do!

Never-Fail Magic Wand

It's not the length of a magician's wand that determines its power, it's the time and care the magician takes in creating this all-important performance tool. I recommend making a wand no longer than you can easily manipulate onstage—or slip in and out of a secret pocket.

WHAT YOU NEED

• 2 rubber furniture leg tips
• 12- to 16-inch (30.5 to 40.6 cm) length of wooden dowel, in a $\frac{1}{2}$-inch (1.3 cm) diameter or larger to fit the furniture leg tips
• saw
• black acrylic paint
• small paintbrush
• glitter
• disposable plate or container
• white craft glue

INSTRUCTIONS

1. Purchase the furniture leg tips, then buy a wooden dowel that fits inside the tips.

2. Use the saw to shorten the dowel to the desired length.

3. Paint the dowel black. Let dry, then give it a second coat for a more finished look.

4. Pour the glitter onto the disposable plate and set it aside.

5. Brush a thick coat of white craft glue on the outside of each furniture tip. Take care not to get glue inside the tips.

6. Roll the tips in the glitter, coating them thoroughly. Set them upright and let dry overnight.

7. Slip the tips on each end of the painted dowel. The removable tips will be very handy when you perform Freya's Floating Ring illusion, as shown on page 80.

Magician's Stage Table

Every self-respecting magician has his own stage table, and many of the illusions in this book call for one. You can use it to put your tools and apparatus on to lay out card tricks. Or you can simply to walk around it to, ahem, misdirect your audience's attention! It can also double as a bedside table in your wizard's chambers.

WHAT YOU NEED

• waist-high, wooden table with square or round top*
• sandpaper
• tack cloth
• matte latex paint in black
• paintbrush
• magical patterns and decorating materials on pages 139 and 141
• acrylic paints in silver, gold, purple, or other wizardly colors
• glitter gel pens
• 2- to 3-inch-wide (5 to 7.6 cm) fringe, long enough to go around the circumference of the table (optional)
• helpful adult wizard
• hot glue gun and glue sticks

*The kind found in flea markets and garage sales. Tables with shelves below the tabletop provide handy storage places for props or the occasional rabbit.

INSTRUCTIONS

1. Sand the table to roughen the surface for painting. Use the tack cloth to wipe away dust.

2. Give the table at least two coats of paint, letting it dry thoroughly between coats. (The matte finish helps conceal any threads you use for levitation illusions.)

3. Follow the decorating instructions on page 139 to embellish the table with magical patterns of your choice, or use the gel pens to draw them freehand. Let dry. (Keep in mind you'll want the drawer to face you, not the audience.)

4. Have an adult wizard use the hot glue gun to adhere the fringe around the bottom edge of the table, positioning the fringe below the drawer if there is one.

Magician's Travel Trunk

Magicians are true world travellers. Even in the 1800s, it was not unheard of to start a tour in America, take the train north to Canada, cross the Atlantic to perform before the crowned heads of Europe, sail to South America, and stop in at islands in the Caribbean! So your trunk should bear travel stickers from the exotic capitals of the world. You'll also want to decorate it with sturdy metal corners and strap it closed with a couple of belts for an authentic touch. (This is also a good way to keep your younger brother out of your stuff.)

WHAT YOU NEED

• corrugated cardboard storage box with removable lid
• acrylic paint in black, green, or other colors of your choice
• paintbrushes
• magical patterns on page 141
• ruler
• pencil
• heavy aluminum foil oven liner
• scissors
• dried-up ball-point pen
• white craft glue
• travel sticker templates on page 21
• white paper
• colored marking pens
• paper hole punch
• 2 belts (optional)

CONJURING EMPEROR PENGUINS & PUFFINS IN ANTARCTICA

VOILÀ! MY OWN PRIVATE ISLAND!

INSTRUCTIONS

1. Paint the trunk a basic black or green for travel, or throw caution to the wind and choose a wizardly color like purple. Let dry, then use a contrasting color to add magical patterns, from page 141, as you're so moved. Let dry.

2. Use the ruler and pencil to measure and mark eight 2 x 6-inch (5 x 15.2 cm) rectangles on the aluminum foil oven liner, then cut them out. Round the ends of each rectangle. Use the ballpoint pen to create several small circles at the ends of each rectangle to make "nail heads." Use the pen to emboss the "nail heads." Rub the centers, then flip over each rectangle and rub around the raised areas. Glue two embossed rectangles on each corner of the trunk.

3. Photocopy the travel sticker templates, and use the marking pens to add color. Cut them out, leaving a half-inch margin around each image. Use the paper hole punch to nip half-circles from the edges, creating "sticker" edges. Glue the stickers to your trunk.

4. Fasten the belts around the trunk.

BON VOYAGE!

Magic Show Poster & Stage Backdrop

Modern-day stage wizards aren't shy about promoting themselves. John Henry Anderson, the Caledonian Conjuror, flew huge balloons over New York City and even gave out pats of butter printed with his name. Now *that's* creativity! Many conjurors also create lavish sets and backdrops for their illusions. Here's how to make your own poster and backdrop. (The backdrop helps render invisible secret threads that are part of some illusions.)

Making the Poster

WHAT YOU NEED

- 11 x 14-inch (27.9 x 35.6 cm) white paper
- access to fonts on a personal computer (optional)
- magical patterns on page 141
- scissors
- glue

INSTRUCTIONS

1. What do the posters of the world's most famous magicians have in common? LARGE WORDS written in ALL CAPITALS, combined with very small words, and at least three or four different fonts (the actual style of the letters). If you have access to a word processor or computer, you can select some fonts you like. Use them to create different parts of the poster. You also can paint them by hand.

2. Your poster needs to tell Who, What, When, and Where. As for Who, the show will be performed by a WORLD-REKNOWNED CONJUROR, STAGE MAGICIAN, & WIZARD OF GREAT REPUTE. That's you! So create a stage name: Robert can become Roberto the Magnifico. Jenny transforms to Geneviève de Magique. GET IT?

3. What about the What? A good magic show poster gives a hint of the wonders to come. It should advertise the EXTRAORDINARY, FANTASTIC, WONDROUS, AND MARVELOUS nature of the magic you'll perform. Page through this book and photocopy some black-and-white illustrations to put in your poster. (In my experience, images of floating ladies and people separated from their heads have always gotten attention.)

4. Add the When and Where you'll perform. At midnight on Tuesday? In a basement, or out in the open in case there are any explosions?

5. Add a strong graphic design to the border and magical patterns.

6. Once everything is glued down, take the poster to a copy shop and have it duplicated. Now paper the town!

NOW SHOWING
IN ROBERT'S GARAGE

THE ALL SEEING

ROBERT-O
the Magnifico

FEATS OF MARVEL
&
MAGIC

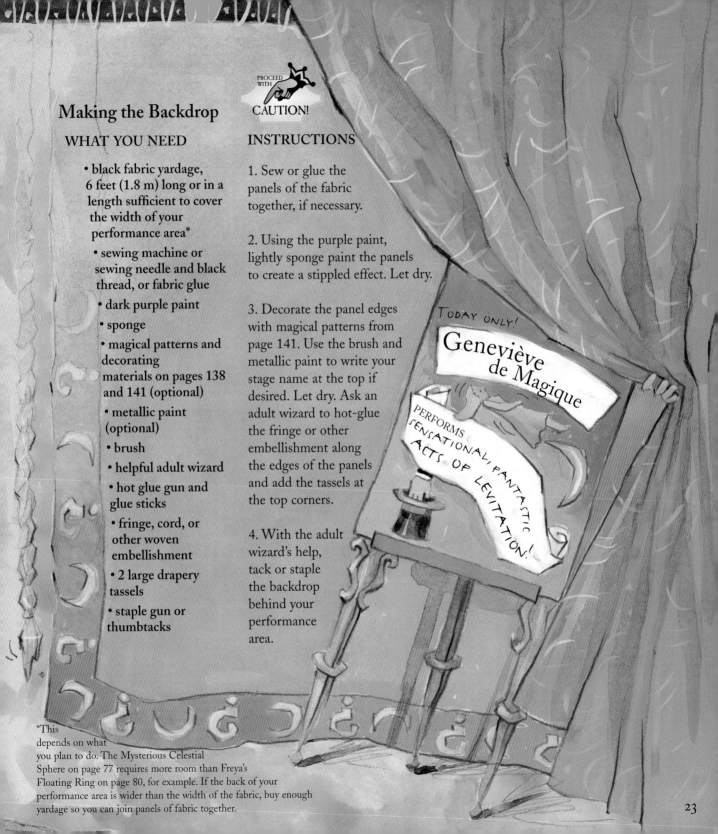

Making the Backdrop

WHAT YOU NEED

- black fabric yardage, 6 feet (1.8 m) long or in a length sufficient to cover the width of your performance area*
- sewing machine or sewing needle and black thread, or fabric glue
- dark purple paint
- sponge
- magical patterns and decorating materials on pages 138 and 141 (optional)
- metallic paint (optional)
- brush
- helpful adult wizard
- hot glue gun and glue sticks
- fringe, cord, or other woven embellishment
- 2 large drapery tassels
- staple gun or thumbtacks

PROCEED WITH CAUTION!

INSTRUCTIONS

1. Sew or glue the panels of the fabric together, if necessary.

2. Using the purple paint, lightly sponge paint the panels to create a stippled effect. Let dry.

3. Decorate the panel edges with magical patterns from page 141. Use the brush and metallic paint to write your stage name at the top if desired. Let dry. Ask an adult wizard to hot-glue the fringe or other embellishment along the edges of the panels and add the tassels at the top corners.

4. With the adult wizard's help, tack or staple the backdrop behind your performance area.

TODAY ONLY!

Geneviève de Magique

PERFORMS SENSATIONAL, FANTASTIC ACTS OF LEVITATION!

*This depends on what you plan to do. The Mysterious Celestial Sphere on page 77 requires more room than Freya's Floating Ring on page 80, for example. If the back of your performance area is wider than the width of the fabric, buy enough yardage so you can join panels of fabric together.

Scholar of Magic Cap

Many people think wizards wear only pointed hats, but that's not true. We like variety in our headgear as much as anyone else does. When Queen Elizabeth I ruled England, my friend Billy Shakespeare was scribbling his plays, and many of them were chock-full of sorcerers and fairies. So many learned people studied magic back in those days that magicians were also called scholars! Caps like this were commonly seen, and they make a dashing addition to your performance wardrobe.

WHAT YOU NEED

- measuring tape
- pencil
- paper
- 1 yard (0.9 m) of craft felt in the color of your choice
- scissors
- straight pins
- sewing needle
- thread to match the craft felt
- decorative ribbon up to 1-1/2 inches (3.8 cm) wide (optional)*
- plume or feather (optional)

*Buy a length equivalent to that of the rectangle created in step 2 below.

INSTRUCTIONS

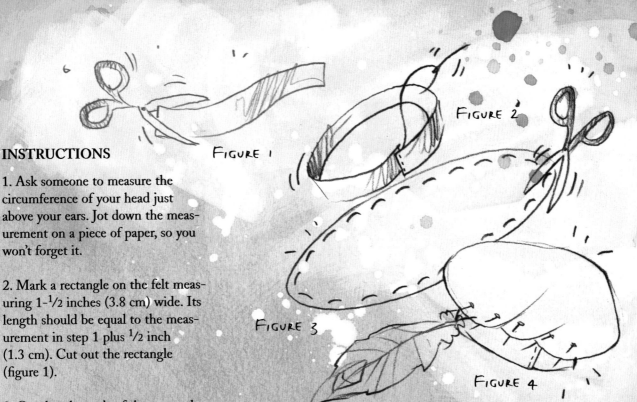

FIGURE 1

FIGURE 2

FIGURE 3

FIGURE 4

1. Ask someone to measure the circumference of your head just above your ears. Jot down the measurement on a piece of paper, so you won't forget it.

2. Mark a rectangle on the felt measuring 1-$\frac{1}{2}$ inches (3.8 cm) wide. Its length should be equal to the measurement in step 1 plus $\frac{1}{2}$ inch (1.3 cm). Cut out the rectangle (figure 1).

3. Overlap the ends of the rectangle about $\frac{1}{4}$ inch (6 mm) to form a circle. Pin it together. Use the needle and thread to sew the overlapped ends together with small straight stitches (figure 2). This will serve as the cap's headband.

4. Set the circular band on a table. Make it as round as possible. Measure the diameter of the circle. Jot down the measurement on a piece of paper.

5. Draw a large circle on the felt; make it three times the diameter you measured in step 4. Cut out the circle.

6. Thread the needle with a long length of thread. Knot the end of the thread. Sew around the edge of the large circle with large, straight basting stitches (figure 3).

7. When you reach the knotted end, gently gather the felt circle, making a "bag." Fit the gathered end of the bag onto the headband, adjusting the gathered felt to make it fit. Pin the headband to the gathered opening (figure 4).

8. Use the needle and a doubled length of thread to sew the headband to the gathered edge.

9. Turn the bag inside out. If desired, sew the decorative ribbon to the outside of the headband, tucking under the raw ends where they join. Use a few stitches to tack the plume to the cap, if desired. Pop the cap on your head.

YOU'RE A SCHOLAR!

25

The Cloak of Mystery

Magicians are a sartorial lot (that means they like to dress to impress). This cape will give you plenty to swirl and twirl, dazzling your audience. It adds mystery to everyday clothes and looks especially impressive when worn with your wizard's robe. It's also got a secret. Pockets are sewn inside to help with vanishing tricks.

WHAT YOU NEED

- measuring tape
- fabric of your choice (see step 1)
- straight pins
- calculator
- pencil or chalk
- ruler
- scissors
- matching thread
- sewing needle or sewing machine
- 1 yard (0.9 m) decorative ribbon

OPTIONAL TOOLS & SUPPLIES
FOR DECORATION

- magical patterns on page 141
- fusible hem tape and webbing
- fabric paints or inks
- rubber stamps
- iron

26

INSTRUCTIONS

1. Decide how long you want your cloak. Use a measuring tape to measure from the base of your neck along your shoulders. Then measure from your shoulder to where you'd like your cape to fall: finger-length, sweeping the floor, or in-between. You will need to buy enough fabric to make a square the same dimension as this measurement. The cloak itself is made from a circle cut from a folded square of fabric. For example, if you need a cloak 36 inches (91 cm) long, you will need to buy 2 yards of fabric at least 72 inches wide. If necessary, you can sew together two widths of yardage. Purchase an extra $1/2$ yard of the fabric for the hood.

2. Fold the square of fabric in half lengthwise, then crosswise. Use straight pins to pin the four layers together.

3. Use a measuring tape to measure around the base of the neck. Use a calculator to divide this measurement by 3.14; then divide the result by 2. This will give you the correct measurement to create the neckline. Mark an arc on the fabric from the folded center using a ruler and pencil or chalk (see figure 1).

4. Mark an arc for the bottom edge of the cloak, measuring from the center fold a distance equal to the length of the cape (see figure 2).

5. Cut on the marked lines through all layers. Cut one folded edge for the center front opening (see figure 3).

6. Hem the bottom edge and opening edges of the cape, if desired.

5. Cut the ribbon into two equal lengths. Use a needle and thread to stitch a length to each side at the neck opening.

6. Cut out 4 x 5 rectangles of fabric to use as pockets. Sew or fuse them to the inside front edges of the cape at waist level. Be sure you match the sides of the fabric, so they will not be noticeable when you open your cape.

7. Decorate the cape as desired if you are using a plain fabric. Just follow the suggestions on page 138.

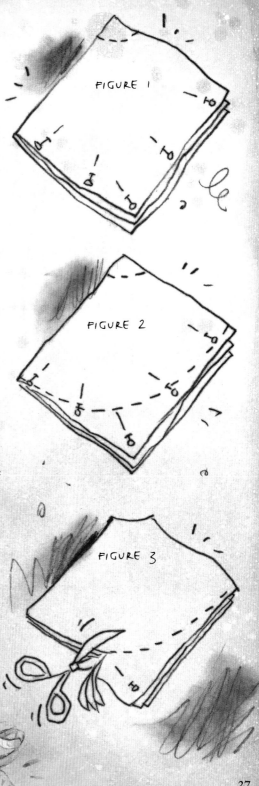

FIGURE 1

FIGURE 2

FIGURE 3

Now-You-See-It, Now-You-Don't Bag

Back in the early 1800s, my English friend Isaac Fawkes was famous for his sleight of hand tricks. After showing people a small, empty bag, he'd make coins, eggs, and even a live chicken appear from inside! This easy-to-make prop is found in every magician's trunk. Make several bags at one time and keep them handy for practicing, vanishing, or transforming objects on the spur of the moment. Then, stupefy your classmates at the lunch table when you make their milk money vanish! (But give it back. Because I said so.)

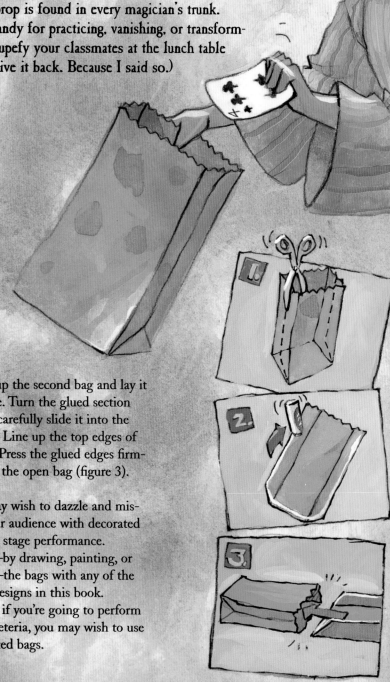

WHAT YOU NEED

- lunch-bag-size paper bags (you'll need two for each bag)
- scissors or craft knife
- pencil
- glue stick
- magical patterns and decorating materials on pages 138 and 141 (optional)

INSTRUCTIONS

1. Open up one paper bag. The fold lines on the sides of the bag will be your guides for cutting the bag. Neatly cut the paper bag along the fold lines indicated by dotted lines (figure 1).

2. Save the smaller section B and recycle section A.

3. Lay section B flat on a table with the folds facing up. Use the glue stick to apply a line of glue on all sides, but not the top (figure 2).

4. Open up the second bag and lay it on its side. Turn the glued section over and carefully slide it into the open bag. Line up the top edges of the bags. Press the glued edges firmly against the open bag (figure 3).

5. You may wish to dazzle and misdirect your audience with decorated bags for a stage performance. Decorate—by drawing, painting, or stamping—the bags with any of the magical designs in this book. However, if you're going to perform in the cafeteria, you may wish to use undecorated bags.

The Trick: Using the Bag to Make Something Vanish

This simple trick is easy to learn. Flat objects like dollar bills, friends' photos, and small coins are easily vanished. Of course, your friends may ask you to make dreaded report cards disappear too!

INSTRUCTIONS

1. Pick up the bag and open it with the secret pocket facing you. Use your left hand to hold the bag with the pocket partially closed. Place your left thumb on the outside of the bag. Your first finger is slipped in the pocket (that keeps the pocket open), and the remaining three fingers are in the main part of the bag (figure 5). Unless your audience is very attentive they won't count your fingers!

2. Keep the open bag slightly tilted away from the audience and towards your body. That will help prevent the audience from seeing the secret pocket.

3. Pick up what you want to vanish (a coin, bill, card, or photo from the audience) with your right hand. Slip the object into the open secret pocket.

5. Place the bag on the table with the pocket facing you and announce you are going to make the object disappear.

6. Pick up the bag with your left hand, this time holding the pocket closed. Speak your magical spell. Grasp the front of the bag with your right hand and tear the front of the bag down to the bottom, showing the empty interior (figure 6).

7. Set the bag aside, away from the audience or crumple it up into a ball and toss it off-stage and perform another trick.

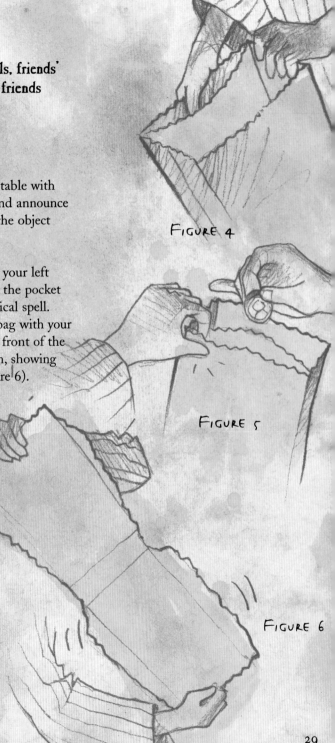

FIGURE 4

FIGURE 5

FIGURE 6

Top Hat

A top hat used to be the mark of a well-dressed gentleman, and magicians cleverly used its generous size to their advantage, hiding doves, rabbits, and whatnot inside. The American magician Richard Potter even fried pancakes inside his topper! But unless you have a time machine, top hats are very hard to find these days. Here's how to make a stage-worthy version of this essential magician's tool.

WHAT YOU NEED

- a helpful friend
- measuring tape
- pencil
- paper
- string
- scissors
- sheets of newspaper
- craft foam in any color*
- white craft glue, or hot glue gun and glue sticks
- masking tape
- paper clips

*You can make a top hat out of stiffened craft felt or poster board if you wish. If you make the hat out of these materials, you will need to add small flaps to attach the crown to the brim.

FIGURE 1   FIGURE 2   FIGURE 3   FIGURE 4   FIGURE 5

INSTRUCTIONS

1. Have your friend measure the circumference of your head slightly above your ears. Write down the measurement.

2. Cut a length of string equal to the measurement in step 1.

3. Lay a sheet of newspaper on a flat surface. Place the string in the center of the sheet and shape it into a rough circle. Use the pencil to trace around the circle (figure 1).

4. Cut out the circle. Set it aside. Now try the piece of newspaper (containing the hole) on your head. Does it fit? You can make it larger by trimming the edge, or you can make it smaller by placing the newspaper on another sheet, tracing inside the circle, and cutting out that circle. When the hole in the newspaper fits your head, you can start making your hat.

5. Lay the newspaper circle on top of the foam, felt, or poster board. Trace around the circle.

6. Make marks about 1 to 1-$\frac{1}{2}$ inches (2.5 to 3.8 cm) around the marked edge of the circle. Connect the marks with a pencil line. Cut out the inner circle first, then the outer circle. The outer circle forms the brim of the top hat (figure 2).

7. Make the hat as tall as you wish, keeping in mind that 12 inches (30.5 cm) is a good height for a top hat. Mark a rectangle on the hat material; it should incorporate the desired height and a width equal to the length of the string you cut in step 2, plus $\frac{1}{2}$ inch (1.3 cm) for overlap. If you're making your hat in another material, add some flaps along the long edge of the rectangle. Draw a line $\frac{1}{2}$ inch (1.3 cm) along the long edge. Cut out the rectangle or the rectangle with the flaps (figure 3).

8. Roll the rectangle into a cylinder and place it on the brim, fitting the cylinder tightly into the inner circle (figure 4). Mark where the ends overlap.

9. Use the craft glue or hot glue to join the overlapped edges of the cylinder. Use the masking tape or paper clips to secure the cylinder until the glue dries.

10. Put a line of glue on the inside edge of the brim and a line of glue on the outside bottom edge of the cylinder. Fit the cylinder into the brim. If needed, use small pieces of the tape to secure the cylinder to the brim. Let the glue dry completely.

11. Use the newspaper circle you made in step 4 to mark a circle on your material. Cut it out.

12. Place the circle on the top of the cylinder (figure 5). Trim it, as needed, to fit on the cylinder. Glue it to the top of the cylinder.

All-Purpose Performance Robe

If this robe could talk, as soon as you walked on stage to begin your show it would announce, Ahem! Pay attention! The person wearing this robe has magical knowledge and powers unknown to YOU, oh mortal! Or something like that. It's designed with handy pockets and secret compartments in the sleeves just right for hiding a bevy of stage bats or a load of coins you've disappeared from audience members. You can also wear it for other wizardly duties and activities.

WHAT YOU NEED

- measuring tape
- fabric yardage (see step 1)*
- pencil, chalk, or other fabric marker
- straight pins
- scissors
- sewing needle and thread to match fabric
- sewing machine (optional)
- fusible webbing
- fusible hem tape or fabric glue (optional)
- fray check or bias tape
- iron
- magical patterns on page 141

*A plain, colorful fabric is easy to decorate if you follow the instructions and patterns in this book. Or you may wish to select a patterned fabric.

INSTRUCTIONS

Making the Robe

1. Ask a fellow magician or sorceress to measure you so that you can determine how much fabric you will need. Stand with your arms down to by your sides. Using the tape measure, ask your friend to measure you from the top of your shoulder to the floor; then add 1 inch (2.5 cm) for the hem. Multiply this measurement by 2 to determine the cut length of fabric needed. Now have your friend measure you from one wrist to the other, across the back of your shoulders, and then add 2 inches (5 cm) for the sleeve hems. This measurement will determine the width of the fabric you will need. Fabrics 45 inches (114.3 cm) wide are usually wide enough for most wizards under the age of 10. Older wizards (or those with long arms) will require wider fabrics or will need to sew on extra fabric for the sleeves. Purchase an extra $^1/_2$ yard (45.7 cm) fabric to create secret pockets on the robe.

Now measure loosely around the base of the neck. Lastly, measure your inside arm length (from wrist to underarm), minus 2 inches (5 cm). Write all these measurements down for future reference.

2. Fold the length of fabric in half, right sides together. Lay the folded fabric flat on a large tabletop or the floor, smoothing out the wrinkles as you work. Pin the bottom edges together in several places.

3. Fold the fabric in half lengthwise (you will have four layers of fabric). Secure the open edges with a few straight pins. See figure 1.

4. Divide the total measurement from wrist to wrist, including the hem allowance, by 2. This measurement is the sleeve length. Measure and mark from the folded edge of the fabric to the sleeve length.

5. Determine how wide you wish the sleeve of the gown to be; 12 to 15 inches (30.5 to 38.1 cm) wide should be sufficient. Make a parallel mark on the unfolded open side with a pencil or chalk to the chosen measurement. Draw from this mark a line equal to the inside arm length running parallel to the top fold. See figure 2.

FIGURE 1

FIGURE 2

33

6. Draw a line from the open edge at the bottom of the fabric to the mark for the inside arm length. See figure 3.

7. For the neckline, divide the neck measurement by 6. Measure and mark a point on the top and side folds from the folded corner. Connect the marks with a curved line to form an arc. See figure 4.

8. Cut through all the layers for the neckline and along the lines marked for the sleeve and sides. See figure 5.

9. Open up the robe and lay it flat. It will look like a T-shape, with the fold at the top.

10. Sew the side and sleeve seams with a $\frac{1}{2}$-inch (1.3 cm) seam allowance, by hand or by machine.

11. You can use fusible hem tape or fabric glue, if you do not wish to sew the hems of the sleeves and the bottom of the robe.

12. Cut a slit from the neckline down the center front of the robe.

13. To finish the edges, use fray check, or attach stitch bias tape by machine or hand.

14. Measure and cut out 8 x 10 inch (20.3 x 25.4 cm) rectangles of fabric. You will need to create two pockets to place at hip level. These pockets will make it easy for you to

make things disappear. If you make additional pockets to place all over the robe they will provide you with even more places to hide things—magic wand, ring, cards, and disappearing handkerchief—and they will confuse your audience. If you're using plain fabric, transfer some of the magical designs on page 141 to the rectangles of fabric before you sew or fuse them to the robe.
Refer to basic decorating instructions on page 138.

15. Measure and cut out two 4 x 5 inch (10.2 x 12.7 cm) rectangles of fabric. Fuse or sew these smaller pockets inside each sleeve about one inch (2.5 cm) from the bottom hem and across the seam line. This will make them easy to reach into and hide small objects.

FIGURE 3

FIGURE 4

FIGURE 5

Thin Air Scarf, & How to Disappear a Coin into Thin Air

In the world of magic, handkerchiefs are not just for noses. With a bit of practice and a flick of your Thin Air Scarf, coins, cards, and rings will seemingly vanish into thin air and mystify your audience. Your stage presence will be hard to ignore if you decorate the scarf to match your cape or robe. Just don't use this magical device on your little sister—your parents might get upset.

WHAT YOU NEED

• 2 printed bandannas or large, plain handkerchiefs
• magical patterns on page 141
• straight pins
• sewing needle or sewing machine
• matching thread
• self-adhesive hook and loop fasteners (small circular ones)
• iron

INSTRUCTIONS

1. Purchase two identical bandannas or plain handkerchiefs. If you are using plain handkerchiefs, decorate them with the patterns of your choice by following the suggestions on page 138.

2. Iron both pieces to eliminate wrinkles. Place one on top of the other, matching the edges. Pin them together with a few straight pins.

3. Sew the pieces together along the sides, leaving approximately 2 inches (5 cm) open at one corner.

4. Create a V-shaped pocket by stitching the pieces together as shown in figure 1. Attach one or two hook and loop fasteners inside the open hem.

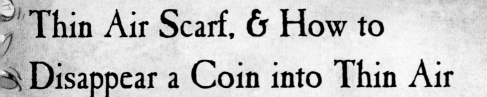

The Trick: Using Your Thin Air Scarf to Disappear a Coin

Use a large coin to practice this simple piece of disappearing magic. The more you practice, the easier the trick will be to execute. As you become adept at making a coin disappear, try other small objects you've "planted" in the audience.

1. Before you perform the trick, slip any coin into secret pocket of the Thin Air Scarf. Hold the scarf by the corners (with the open pocket up!) and display both sides to your audience. Ask a member of the audience if you may borrow THE SAME TYPE of coin as you drape the scarf and rest the hidden coin on your open left palm (figure 1).

2. Place the borrowed coin on top of the hidden coin. Grasp the stack of the hidden and the borrowed coin with the fingers of your right hand (figure 2). Turn the scarf and held coins upside down so that the scarf falls over your opened right palm. The borrowed coin will fall into your palm and be hidden by the scarf.

3. Grasp the coin hidden in the scarf with the fingers of your left hand. At the same time, slightly curl the fingers of your right hand. Shift the hidden coin on your palm, catching it in the groove between your palm and fingers. This is called the finger-palm position (figure 3).

4. Ask a spectator to grasp their coin (really the hidden one) through the scarf with their fingers. As they do this, you will curl the fingers of the right hand over the hidden coin. Bring your right hand down to your side. You can slip the coin into one of your pockets as you misdirect the attention of the audience,

5. When you are ready to make the hidden coin disappear, grasp the bottom corner of the scarf, utter any of the magic words on page 37, wave your opposite hand, and give the scarf a sharp tug. Pull the scarf towards you.

6. Grasp the scarf by two corners (with the open pocket up) and display the empty scarf to your amazed audience. Proceed with the next trick in your magic act. Later on, as you reach into your pocket for a wand or cards, "discover" the borrowed coin and return it to the proper owner.

Useful Magical Commands

When you make magic, it makes sense that you need a magical command or two. But I'm not saying you have to go as far as the Greek wizard Apollonius. Legend says he could speak all languages, including those of animals and birds. And you don't have to copy the South American wizards whose spells turned into human form to carry out orders!

Some commands have been well-known to wizards for centuries, while others may be new to you (including the ones that I invented myself, thank you very much). You can also teach a word to your audience and ask them to "help the magic happen" by shouting out the word when you raise your hand. (This technique is also useful for misdirecting the attention of your audience at a crucial point of an illusion. See page 14 for more practical performance tips.)

Sator Arepo Tenet Opera Rotas! Milon Irago Lamal Ogari Nolim! During the Middle Ages, many wizards used palindromes, which are words or phrases that read the same forward and backward. They sound very impressive when you use them as a magical incantation while performing a trick onstage. Print one on your stage backdrop (page 23) for an air of mystery.

CIGAM EB EREHT TEL!

Try writing down a magical phrase—even your own name—but in reverse, then say it out loud. Sounds magical, yes? Or, hold the writing up to a mirror and copy the reflection to create an instant magical inscription in a secret language.

I COMMAND YOU!

Magic is about making things happen, right? Here are some useful commands of mine. Try combining them to create a phrase. And there is certainly no rule that you can't make up your own. My magician friends, such as Signor Ochus Bochus, came up with some, shall we say, highly imaginative commands.

Levitatus! [leh-vuh-TAH-tuss] Rise!

Flotatus! [flow-TAH-tuss] Float!

Fugit! [FEW-jit] Fly!

Gravitus Desistas! [grah-VEE-tuss duh-SISS-tuss] Sink!

Apparere! [ah-pah-RERE-ee] Appear!

Disapparere! [DISS-ah-pah-RERE-ee] Disappear!

Citatia! [sih-TAH-tee-ah] Come here!

Accelera! [ack-SELL-UR-ah] Hurry up!

Capta! [KAP-tuh] Grab!

Repitatus! [reh-puh-TAH-tuss] Again!

Abracadabra! See page 128 for my explanation of this famous phrase.

Shazaam, Alakazaam! The meaning has been lost with time, but it sounds good.

Mind Reader's Ring, and the Transparent Card Trick

Every stage wizard worth his robe should have a giant gem sparkling on his finger. So who'll be the wiser if your ring has, shall we say, a secret ingredient that gives you the ability to "see through" the back of a playing card?

WHAT YOU NEED

• plain band ring in size to fit the index finger of your non-dominant hand (for example, if you're right-handed, it should fit your left finger)
• cyanoacrylate glue
• small dental mirror, about $1/2$ inch (1.3 cm) in diameter
• giant plastic jewel
• deck of playing cards
• clear glass tumbler big enough to hold the (upright) deck of cards

INSTRUCTIONS

1. Glue the plastic jewel on one side of the ring and let dry.

2. Glue the mirror on the opposite side of the ring with the reflective side facing out. Let dry.

The Trick: The Transparent Card

1. Put the ring on the index finger of your left hand, and keep the mirror hidden from the audience. This shouldn't be hard, if the jewel on your ring is big and gaudy enough!

2. Hand the pack of cards to an audience member to be examined and shuffled thoroughly.

3. Use your left hand to hold out the glass tumbler and have the spectator place the deck of cards in the tumbler so the back of the cards face you.

4. Use the fingertips of your left hand to hold the tumbler of cards almost up to eye level. Position your left index finger so the mirror reflects the card's suit and number of the card at the front of the deck (which faces the audience).

5. One by one, use your right hand to lift up the front card so the audience can see it. Without turning the card around, call out the card's suit (hearts, spades, clubs, or diamonds) and number, which you have already spotted thanks to the secret mirror. Continue doing this through the whole deck. Leaping wizards! As far as your audience can tell, you can see through each card!

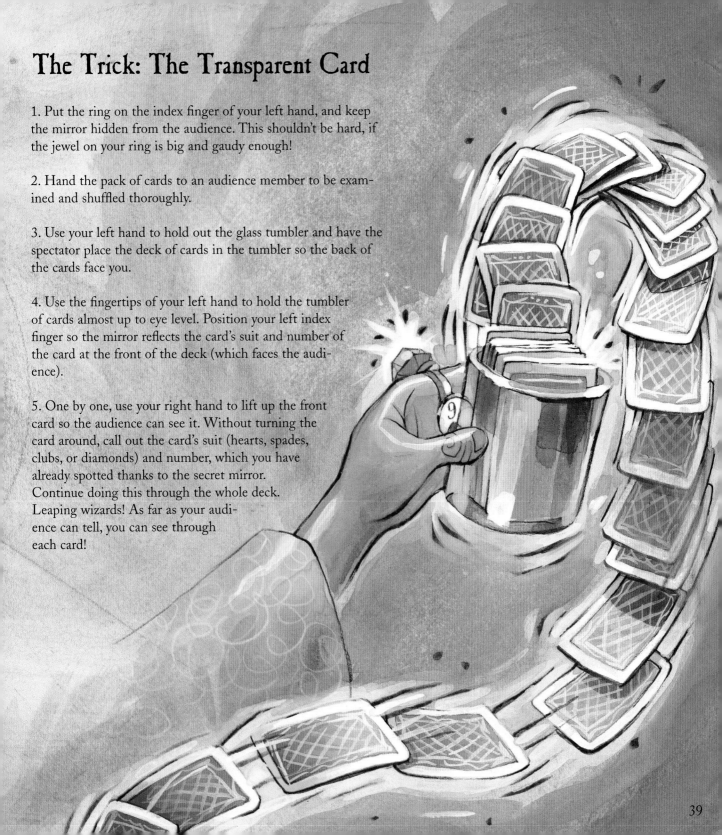

Chapter 3

NOW YOU SEE IT, NOW YOU DON'T

APPEARING & DISAPPEARING
ACTS & ILLUSIONS

Making things appear and disappear is as basic as wizard craft gets. I advise you to master my secrets of the Vanishing Wand and Disappearing Magic Ring (pages 42 and 44). Ever heard of putting the *fluence* on an audience? In the magic trade, that means using the spell of your personality and onstage demeanor to make people see what you want them to see. Not many people know its origins. A long time ago, the Little People cast enchantments called fairy glamour. You know, a hag would disguise herself so a mortal saw only a lovely damsel. Or a prince appeared to be a frog, that sort of thing. And speaking of frogs and other animal familiars, I'll teach you how to make yours appear from nowhere in my Owl from a Box trick (page 48).

Two-Way Vanishing Wand Trick

Being a wizard, you have of course used your wand to summon helpful genies or to make a nasty dwarf disappear. Here's how to make a wand that appears and disappears at your command. This is a good illusion to use as the opener of a performance.

WHAT YOU NEED

• 2 sheets of 8-$\frac{1}{2}$ x 11-inch (cm) white typing paper

• 2 wooden dowels, $\frac{1}{2}$ inch (1.3 cm) in diameter, one dowel 1 foot (cm) long and one dowel 2 inches (5 cm) long

• white craft glue

• pencil

• ruler

• black acrylic paint

• paintbrush

• small, waist-high table (see page 19 for Magician's Stage Table)

• sheet of newspaper or colored gift wrap

INSTRUCTIONS

1. Tightly roll one sheet of the white paper around the longer dowel (figure 1), and glue down the edge. Repeat with the second sheet of paper and the shorter dowel. Let dry.

2. Use the pencil to push the short dowel all the way to one end of its paper tube (figure 2).

3. Use the ruler to measure 1 inch (2.5 cm) from each end of each wand, and make light pencil marks at that point.

4. Paint the middle section of each tube black, leaving the 1-inch (1.3 cm) ends unpainted and white. You now have two identical wands: one solid and one mostly hollow.

The Performance

1. Position the table in front of your audience, and place the sheet of newspaper on top. Leave the room.

2. Hide the solid wand inside your robe. Holding the hollow wand between the fingertips of both of your hands, walk back to the table in front of your audience.

3. As you tap the wooden end of the hollow wand on the table, announce, "For anyone who doubts that I am a true wizard, take heed and watch closely!" Pointing the wand upward, say dismissively,

"Anyone can hide this magic wand by wrapping it in this newspaper." Pick up the paper and wrap it around the wand (figure 3). "But can you make it disappear?" Bend the rolled newspaper (and wand) in the middle (figure 4), and tear it into pieces, wadding them up and hiding the piece of wood in a wad. Reach into your robe and say, "But you know how it is with magic wands." Whip out the solid wand from your robe (figure 5) and rap it repeatedly on the table while continuing, "They have a way of reappearing!" Bow and exit!

Disappearing Magic Ring Trick

Jules de Rovère was an elegant French aristocrat who, being a teensy bit eccentric, liked to hang around magic shops in Paris and perform sleight-of-hand tricks. He coined one of my favorite words, *prestidigitation*, to describe how a mortal magician uses hidden hand movements to create illusions. You'll do a bit of that with the palming techniques used in this trick, and make a wizard's ring as well.

WHAT YOU NEED

- 2 flat, plain, identical rings made from hard plastic in a size that fits the ring finger of your non-dominant hand*
- pencil
- coping saw
- fine sandpaper or scouring pad
- 2 identical, large flat marble or plastic jewels
- jewelry glue
  - plain handkerchief or Thin Air Scarf (page 35)
  - an assistant from the audience

*If you're right-handed, it should fit your left ring finger. Vice versa if you're a lefty.

INSTRUCTIONS

1. Slip one of the rings on your finger, and use the pencil to make a mark on both sides of the ring where it begins to curve around the finger.

2. Use the coping saw to cut off the bottom part of the ring at the points you marked. Use the sandpaper to smooth any rough edges.

3. Glue a jewel to the top of each ring. Let dry.

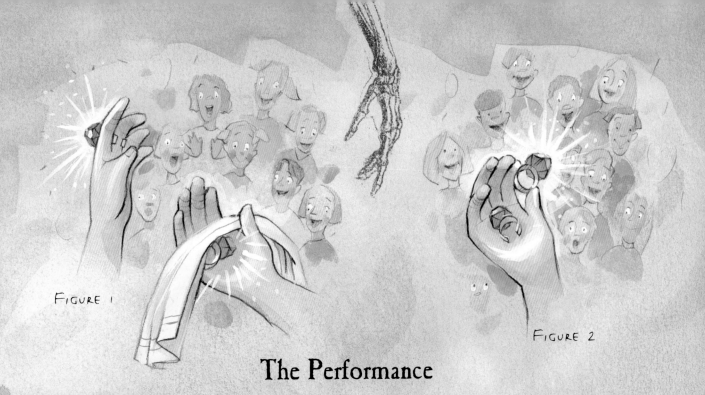

FIGURE 1

FIGURE 2

The Performance

1. Now you're ready to perform. While holding the scarf with your right hand and palming the uncut ring in the same hand, display the half-ring to them, with your fingers positioned so the cutaway is hidden (figure 1). At the same time say, "Behold my Disappearing Magic Ring, handed down to me from ancient wizards past! It will now adorn my finger." Slide the ring onto your left hand, keeping the fingers together to hide the cutaway.

2. Call for a volunteer from the audience. Explain that he or she must grasp the end of the finger wearing the ring and not let go, whatever happens.

3. While the volunteer hangs on, announce, "Such a magnificent ring needs darkness for its magic to work," and quickly drape the scarf over the left hand.

4. Here's the part you should have practiced repeatedly. Say, "*Pesto Presto Prestidigitation!* Ow! Powerful magic like this tickles, especially when something solid moves through you! I'm glad the jewel wasn't any bigger!" At the same time you're speaking, bring your right hand up under the scarf, quickly move the palmed, whole ring to your right fingertips, and use the undersides of a couple of fingers from your right hand to grasp the gem of the half-ring, remove it from your left finger, and palm it.

5. As you announce, "Aha! The genius of the ages has once again served me. Behold!" display the whole ring to the audience (figure 2). Hand it to your volunteer (keeping the palmed ring hidden) and say, "Take a look at this treasure. Display its brilliance all who are here, but don't let go of my finger just yet!" During the brief time the audience is looking at the volunteer, drop your right hand to your side and slip the half-ring into the pocket of your robe.

6. Use your right hand to whip away the scarf. Your left ring finger is empty. The ring has vanished!

The Card that Changes Its Spots

I remember when every self-respecting street magician back in the Middle Ages performed this illusion using a small wooden paddle instead of a card. The key to this trick is to precisely place your fingers over spots or empty places on the card. As you turn the card, your audience will think it has four sides! They'll see one spot, then four spots, then three spots, then six spots, all on a two-sided card! Impossible? Not at all. It's magic! Helped by lots of practice in front of a mirror, of course.

What You Need

• piece of white posterboard, 2-3/4 x 4-1/2 inches (cm)
• 7 large, self-adhesive colored paper dots*
*available in office supply stores

Instructions

1. Apply the dots to both sides of the posterboard as shown in figure 1.

2. Refer to figures 2 through 4 while reading the following directions and practicing in front of a mirror.

The Performance

1. Show the two-dot side (figure 2) to your audience (the mirror), with the lower dot hidden by your fingers. The audience will "see" a card that has one dot in the middle.

2. Flip the card over to display the five-dot side, being careful to cover the middle dot (figure 3). But the card you're showing has four dots—or at least the audience thinks so.

3. Turn the card from front to back AND reverse it top to bottom to show the two-dot side to the audience—but make sure your fingers cover the empty space at the bottom (figure 4). Presto, the side that had one dot now has three!

4. Again, turn the card from front to back and reverse it top to bottom, so the five-dot side faces the audience while your fingers cover the empty space at the side (figure 5). Change-O, the side that had four dots now has six!

FIGURE 1

FIGURE 2

FIGURE 3

FIGURE 4

FIGURE 5

47

Owl Familiar from a Box

If your trusty familiar would rather not be crammed into a box, here's how to materialize a stand-in from thin air. Or at least your audience will think so! Use an owl, rabbit, hedgehog, or another compactly shaped stuffed animal.

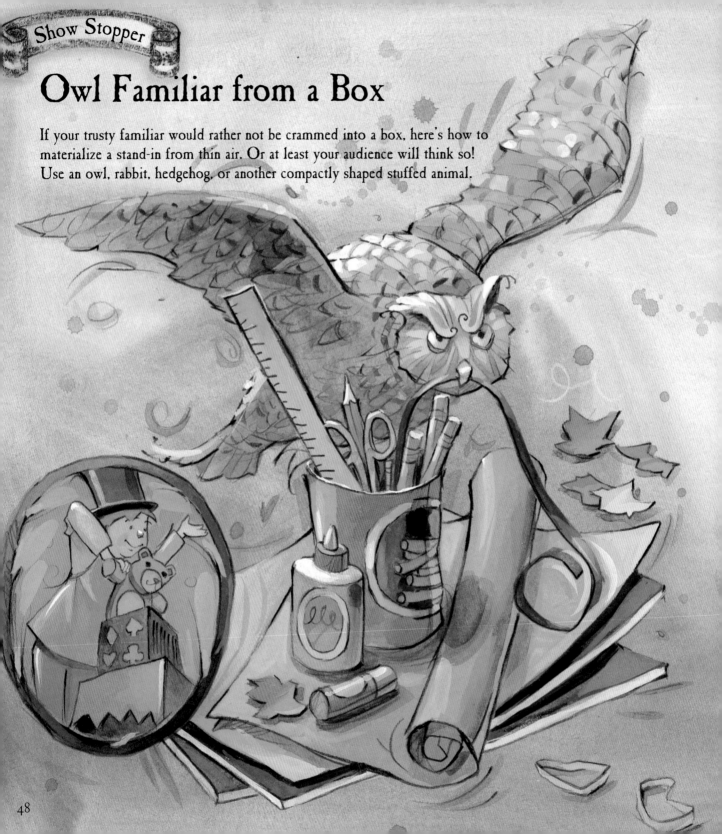

WHAT YOU NEED

• small, stuffed animal approximately 8 inches (20.3 cm) tall
• sheet of black foam core board*
• sheet of black poster board
• sheet of poster board in any bright color
• black cloth or plastic tape
• scraps of brightly colored paper (optional)
• white craft glue
• glue stick
• metal-edged ruler
• pencil
• scissors
• helpful adult wizard
• craft knife
• rubber bands

*available at most craft or framing stores

INSTRUCTIONS

1. Measure the exact height of the stuffed animal and write down the measurement.

2. Add an extra $\frac{1}{2}$ inch (1.3 cm) to the animal's height and mark it on the black poster board. Make another mark at the same height and 15 inches (38.1 cm) away from the first. Use a ruler to connect the marks with a straight line. Cut out this rectangle.

3. Use the poster board to make a cylinder that fits comfortably around the animal without being too snug. Glue the end of the board to the cylinder. Slip the rubber bands around it to hold the cylinder in place until the glue dries.

4. Measure and mark a rectangle on the colored poster board. This rectangle should be 1 inch (2.5 cm) longer and taller than the black rectangle you made in step 2. Cut it out. Form this rectangle into a cylinder that will fit comfortably around the black cylinder. It needs to be wide enough to slip easily over the black cylinder without touching it (figure 1). Glue the end of the board to the cylinder, secure it with rubber bands, and let the glue dry.

5. Measure and mark four squares on the black foam core board. The sides of each square should be equal to the height of the black cylinder.

With the help of an adult wizard, cut out the squares with a sharp craft knife. Use the metal-edged ruler as a straight edge as you cut. Set three squares aside (figure 2).

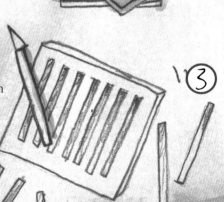

49

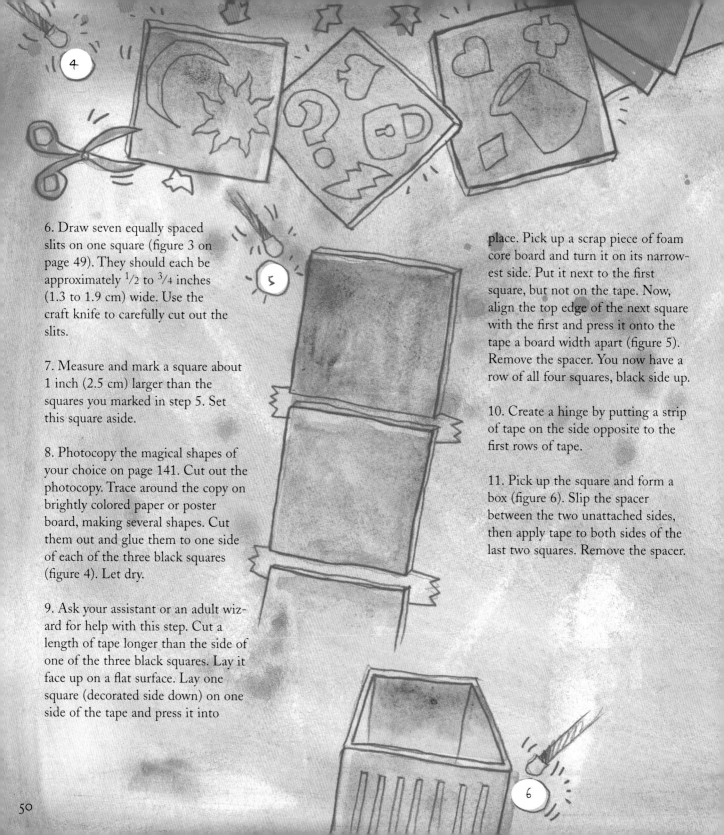

6. Draw seven equally spaced slits on one square (figure 3 on page 49). They should each be approximately ¹/₂ to ³/₄ inches (1.3 to 1.9 cm) wide. Use the craft knife to carefully cut out the slits.

7. Measure and mark a square about 1 inch (2.5 cm) larger than the squares you marked in step 5. Set this square aside.

8. Photocopy the magical shapes of your choice on page 141. Cut out the photocopy. Trace around the copy on brightly colored paper or poster board, making several shapes. Cut them out and glue them to one side of each of the three black squares (figure 4). Let dry.

9. Ask your assistant or an adult wizard for help with this step. Cut a length of tape longer than the side of one of the three black squares. Lay it face up on a flat surface. Lay one square (decorated side down) on one side of the tape and press it into

place. Pick up a scrap piece of foam core board and turn it on its narrowest side. Put it next to the first square, but not on the tape. Now, align the top edge of the next square with the first and press it onto the tape a board width apart (figure 5). Remove the spacer. You now have a row of all four squares, black side up.

10. Create a hinge by putting a strip of tape on the side opposite to the first rows of tape.

11. Pick up the square and form a box (figure 6). Slip the spacer between the two unattached sides, then apply tape to both sides of the last two squares. Remove the spacer.

THE TRICK:
How to Materialize the Owl from the Box

Assemble this illusion on your magician's table before you start your act, or have your assistant bring it onstage at your command.

FIGURE 10

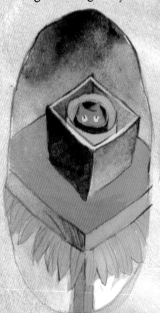

FIGURE 7

FIGURE 8

FIGURE 9

produce an owl (or whatever animal you've chosen) from thin air.

1. Place the box on the larger black square. Slip the colored cylinder inside the box and the black cylinder inside the colored cylinder. Place the stuffed animal inside the black cylinder (figure 7). Place the assembly with the slotted side facing the audience. Have your magic wand handy.

2. Announce that you are going to

3. Pick up the black box. Look at the audience through the bottom (figure 8). You can even flatten the box if you wish to further add to the mystery of the trick. Then, replace the box over the cylinder on the black square with the slotted side facing the audience.

4. Lift the colored cylinder out of the box. Show the audience that it,

too, is empty by looking through it. The audience will not be able to see the smaller cylinder because the color matches the color of the box (figure 9).

5. Replace the colored cylinder in the box over the black cylinder.

6. Wave your magic wand over the box with a flourish and speak a magic charm (see page 37). Carefully reach inside the black cylinder and produce the stuffed animal (figure 10). Take care not to pull out the black cylinder!

FAMOUS Disappearing Illusions

Disappearing acts always delight. (However, young magician, I do *not* recommend trying to spirit away another wizard's beard. One young student of mine tried it, and he ended up dragging around a floor-length beard of his own for days. Served him right. I should have turned him into a hair ball.)

Disappearing magic can be performed around a table or on a massive scale in front of an audience in a theater. The famous magician Alexander Hermann liked to make things vanish from the dinner table, especially glasses full of wine. I once saw him snatch someone's glass and throw it into the air. It disappeared!

If it weren't for the ever-useful Third Eye that Fatima the Gypsy Queen sewed on my wizard's hat, I wouldn't have known Hermann's secret. He hid a clear plastic top in the palm of his hand, then snapped it over the rim of the glass as he grabbed it. Pretending to throw the glass high into the air—as dinner guests goggled—he actually flipped it around his hand and palmed the base of the glass. By the time everyone looked down, there sat Hermann, an innocent expression on his face, drumming his fingers on the table's edge. Meanwhile, the glass dangled upside down from his palm, hidden from view. Of course, he always rematerialized the glass and gave it back.

Howard Thurston loved to make things disappear onstage: girls, pianos, even automobiles. After shutting an assistant in a mummy case onstage, he hauled it up by ropes so it dangled overhead, then lowered it down again. Case empty, girl gone! In his Phantom Piano act, he did the same with a pianist and her piano! After they disappeared, the music mysteriously continued. Creepy. (Howard's secret: The piano was a shell that folded flat while the music came from a piano offstage).

Sometimes bigger isn't better. Carter the Great wanted to vanish something big, too, and he chose an elephant. The feat required raising the animal on a platform above the stage and covering it with curtains.

But the elephant refused to stay put while it was cranked above the stage (sensible beast!), and Carter made four assistants disappear instead.

I have to tip my sorcerer's hat to my friend Jasper Maskelyne for the most incredible disappearing acts I've seen in my 600 years. He made a fleet of battleships float up the River Thames in England, or so it seemed (he really used mirrors and a small model). The Royal Engineers Camouflage Corps of the British Army immediately sent him to Egypt (World War II was on, chaps), where Jasper made the Suez Canal disappear, all 100 miles (160 km) of it! He used a series of spinning strobe lights to misdirect bombers trying to destroy the canal,

and they were literally unable to find it. While in Egypt, Jasper also disappeared the harbor of Alexandria and the entire British Eighth Army, tricking the enemy into thinking they were somewhere else.

But I do not recommend that you follow the example of amateur magician Doc Nixon, who took "Now you see it, now you don't" to the extreme. He disappeared in 1939. Did he abandon his worldly life to become a Tibetan monk, as some said, or did he join the great Merlin, who also vanished without a trace?

chapter 4
TRANSFIGURATION & SHAPE-SHIFTING

If you know your wizard history, you're familiar with my dear friend Merlin's ability to shape-shift into different animal and human forms. I suggest you master some shapeshifting magic of your own. The Frenchman Buatier de Kolta (Boo Boo to his friends) used to shrink playing cards until, Pouf!, they disappeared, then he enlarged them to a size fit for giants. You can fit your own body through a playing card—no kidding—with my Magical Cutting of the Cards trick on page 64. I always liked magic with edible results, too. See Sucre Bleu's After Dinner Entertainment on page 68 for how to change confetti into delicious candy.

BON APPETIT!

The Impossible Knot

Did you ever hear the story of King Gordias, who invented the most incredibly complicated knot ever seen that no one could figure out? (Actually, his chief sorcerer did it.) When Alexander the Great was visiting, he heard an oracle prophesy that whoever undid the famous Gordian knot would become the next ruler of Asia. Alexander drew his sword and hacked right through the rope! He eventually became ruler of most of the civilized world. Here's another knotty conundrum to astonish your friends. How can you tie a knot in a handkerchief without letting go of the ends? Like Alexander's solution, the secret is elegantly simple.

WHAT YOU NEED

• 1 piece of fabric 24 inches (61 cm) square, or Thin Air Scarf (page 35)

INSTRUCTIONS

1. To start your performance, tell the story of King Gordias. Then, while flapping your scarf in the air, say, "And I, too, will demonstrate to you how I can tie an impossible knot. . . without letting go of the ends of this handkerchief!"

2. Fold your arms, as shown above, then take hold of two opposing ends of the handkerchief.

3. Without letting go of the handkerchief, unfold your arms.

4. Now collect the wizard gold owed you by anyone (foolish mortal!) who bet you couldn't do it!

Wizard of Oz Balloon Magic

Sometimes magic makes noise. *Blam!* Your audience will be dumb-founded as they watch you pop a balloon, revealing another one inside in a color they randomly selected beforehand. Like my acquaintance Professor Marvel in the Land of Oz, I've always been partial to balloon rides. Even if his magical powers were a bit questionable, I named this trick in honor of my famous fellow wizard.

WHAT YOU NEED

PROCEED WITH CAUTION!

- 1 clean, empty frozen orange juice can, with lid removed
- acrylic paints in wizardly colors of your choice
- paintbrush
- decorative patterns of your choice on page 141 (optional)
- hammer
- nails
- 4 strips of scrap wood, 5 inches (12.7 cm), 4 inches (10.2 cm), 3 inches (7.6 cm), and 2 inches (5 cm) respectively
- 1 piece of scrap board, 1 foot (30.5 cm) long
- 3 wooden dowels, each 3 feet (0.9 m) long, $1/8$-inch (3 mm) in diameter
- handsaw
- sharpened pencil with eraser on the end
- helpful adult wizard
- safety goggles
- straight pin
- wire cutters
- electric drill, with bit matching diameter of straight pin
- cyanoacrylate glue
- pliers
- balloons in rich blue, purple, and green, plus an equal number in red
- string or fishing line
- scissors
- Magician's Stage Table (page 19) or another table

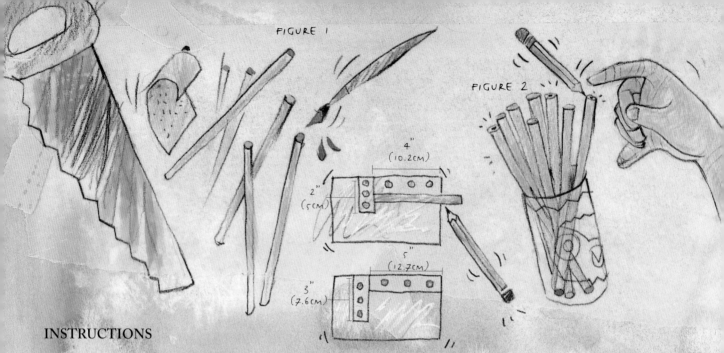

FIGURE 1

FIGURE 2

4"
(10.2CM)

2"
(5CM)

5"
(12.7CM)

3"
(7.6CM)

INSTRUCTIONS

1. Paint the empty frozen orange juice can, let dry, then add a second coat and let dry. Add decorative patterns, if desired, by painting freehand or through a stencil.

2. To aid in precisely cutting the dowels to 5-inch (12.7 cm) lengths, you'll need to create a jig. (It's very important that the dowels are exactly the same length.) Nail the 5-inch and 3-inch (12.7 and 7.6 cm) strips at right angles to each other on the 1-foot (0.9 m) board.

3. Place the dowel against the 5-inch (12.7 cm) side of the jig, with its end butted against the shorter piece, and use the saw to cut off 5-inch (12.7 cm) sections of dowel (figure 1). Repeat with the remaining dowels.

4. Create another jig, this time with the 4-inch and 2-inch (10.2 and 5 cm) strips of scrap wood. Place each dowel in the jig as shown, holding the pencil at the end. Turn the dowel, making a pencil mark all the way around that's 1 inch (2.5 cm) from the end (figure 1).

5. Set aside three of the marked dowels. Paint the ends green, yellow, and purple respectively, and use the pencil to make a small but visible dot on each unpainted end (figure 2). Use red paint on the ends of the rest of the dowels, but DON'T make pencil marks on them. Let dry.

6. Get an adult to help you with this part. Select the dowel with the purple end. Wearing the safety goggles, use the wire cutters to cut off the head of the straight pin. Either using a drill bit that matches the diameter of the pin, or using the pin itself as a bit, slowly drill a 1/4-inch-deep

(6 mm) hole in the end of the dowel. Keep the bit as straight as possible. Be sure to remember that the purple colored dowel contains the pin!

7. Apply a teeny bit of the glue to one end of the pin, and use the pliers to push the pin, gluey end first, into the hole. Use the wire cutters to cut off some of the protruding end of the pin so only 1/32 inch (0.8 mm) sticks out.

8. Use the eraser end of the pencil to push a red balloon inside each balloon of a different color, being careful not to tear or puncture the balloon. To prepare the doubled balloons for the performance, first blow up the inner red balloon, then knot or tie it closed with a piece of string. Blow a little more air into the outer balloon, and tie it around the inner balloon with string (figure 3).

FIGURE 4

FIGURE 3

The Illusion

Changing the Balloon Color on Command

1. Put all the painted dowels, colored ends down, in the can. Set the dowels and blown-up balloons on a table. You're ready to perform! (You've practiced, right?)

2. Open the performance by talking about the Wizard of Oz and how fond wizards are of balloon rides. Then say, "And now I'd like to show you my magic sticks." Pick up the container full of dowels and say, "The end of each magic stick is colored." Pulling out one of the sticks marked with the pencil dot, say (if you've pulled out the yellow one), "This one is yellow." Lay it on the table. Remix the sticks, pushing them around while keeping them in the container. Then repeat the process with a second marked dowel, displaying and announcing its color

to the audience. Repeat for the third marked dowel. By now, the yellow, purple, and green dowels should be lying on the table. Don't let your audience examine them closely!

3. Bring the container of dowels to someone in the audience, asking her to "mix" the sticks without taking them out of the container. Have her select a stick and take it out of the container, but tell her to hide the color of the tip from you and the audience.

4. Set the container back on the table. If you're right-handed, use your left hand to pick up a purple balloon by its tied end from the table. With your right hand, pick up the purple stick lying on the table. Say to the audience, "Here is a pur-

ple balloon and one of my magic colored sticks. My charming audience member has chosen another stick, but no one knows what color it is. We do know that she doesn't have one of the colors I already chose. And we also know she doesn't have the purple stick, which I took out. Now, will the lady please remove her hand from the end of the stick and display its color!" After she shows the red end, say, "The color is red! Please watch the balloon!"

5. Shout, *Coloris magnificum!* Poke the purple end of the stick against the purple balloon. Bang! The tiny pinpoint should have penetrated the outer, purple balloon while leaving the inner balloon intact (figure 4). You're now holding a red balloon in your hand!

TAKE A BOW.

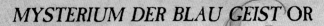

MYSTERIUM DER BLAU GEIST OR

The Mystery of the Blue Ghost

Long ago in Berlin, a German sorceress named Lola showed me this trick. I'll *never* forget her. (Er, I mean, I think she stole it from a certain Professor Rath. Remind me to tell you about her when you're older. Not now.) You can entertain your audience with the story of the blue ghost. Viewers simply will not understand how a colored wooden block can go where it's not supposed to be.

IT'S MAGIC!

WHAT YOU NEED

- ruler
- pencil
- 1 wood dowel, 1-inch (2.5 cm) diameter, 13 inches (33 cm) long
- handsaw
- sandpaper
- blue acrylic paint
- paintbrush
- newspaper
- scissors
- cellophane tape
- brightly colored or patterned wrapping or construction paper
- glue stick
- 1 piece of balsa wood, $1/4$ inch (6 mm) thick, 3 x 6 inches (7.6 x 15.2 cm)
- rubber bands

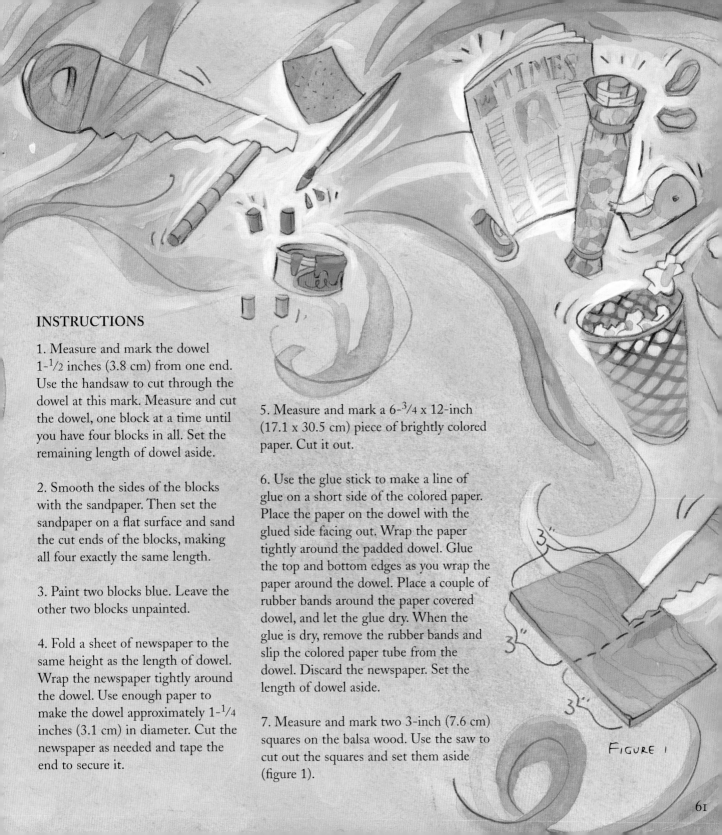

INSTRUCTIONS

1. Measure and mark the dowel 1-$^1/_2$ inches (3.8 cm) from one end. Use the handsaw to cut through the dowel at this mark. Measure and cut the dowel, one block at a time until you have four blocks in all. Set the remaining length of dowel aside.

2. Smooth the sides of the blocks with the sandpaper. Then set the sandpaper on a flat surface and sand the cut ends of the blocks, making all four exactly the same length.

3. Paint two blocks blue. Leave the other two blocks unpainted.

4. Fold a sheet of newspaper to the same height as the length of dowel. Wrap the newspaper tightly around the dowel. Use enough paper to make the dowel approximately 1-$^1/_4$ inches (3.1 cm) in diameter. Cut the newspaper as needed and tape the end to secure it.

5. Measure and mark a 6-$^3/_4$ x 12-inch (17.1 x 30.5 cm) piece of brightly colored paper. Cut it out.

6. Use the glue stick to make a line of glue on a short side of the colored paper. Place the paper on the dowel with the glued side facing out. Wrap the paper tightly around the padded dowel. Glue the top and bottom edges as you wrap the paper around the dowel. Place a couple of rubber bands around the paper covered dowel, and let the glue dry. When the glue is dry, remove the rubber bands and slip the colored paper tube from the dowel. Discard the newspaper. Set the length of dowel aside.

7. Measure and mark two 3-inch (7.6 cm) squares on the balsa wood. Use the saw to cut out the squares and set them aside (figure 1).

FIGURE 1

THE ILLUSION:

IT'S ALIVE!
Making the Blue Ghost Move

WHAT YOU NEED

- paper tube
- blocks
- tray

INSTRUCTIONS

1. The magic of this illusion lies in the paper tube and in controlling what your audience sees. Before performing, practice with the tube and blocks in front of a mirror. Stack the four blocks and place the tube over them.

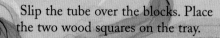

Master this movement, and you're ready to perform!

2. Before the performance, prepare the trick on a flat tray by stacking two unpainted blocks with the two blue blocks on top (figure 2).

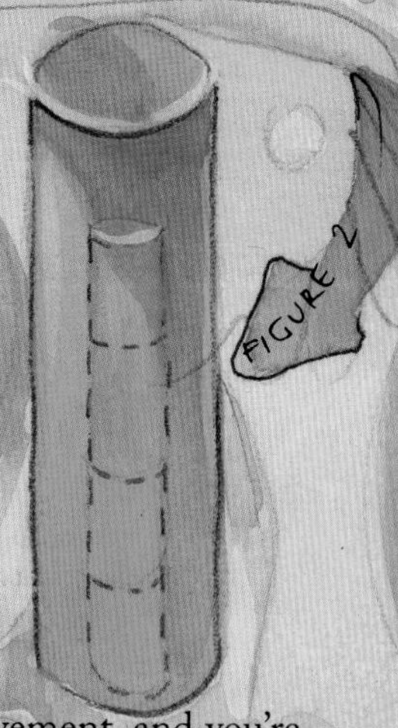

Lightly squeeze the top of the tube, gripping the top block. Carefully lift the tube (containing the hidden block) straight up without toppling the three remaining blocks. Then hold the tube at an angle facing the mirror (your audience) so the bottom of the tube is partially visible and looks empty.

Slip the tube over the blocks. Place the two wood squares on the tray.

3. To open the performance, tell your audience that when you performed in the castle of Ludwig, the Mad King of Bavaria, you met *der blau geist* [durr BLAW GUYST]. The blue ghost taught you its secrets of shape-shifting and passing through solid stone walls. Then say, "And now, with the help of the blue ghost, I will show you how these feats are done!" Grasp the top block, hold it, and raise the paper tube to show only three blocks. Hold the tube so the audience can see partway into the tube. Holding the tube and hidden block, use your free hand to place the three blocks in a row on the tray. Pick up the blue block and tell the audience, "This is the blue ghost, who can change shape at will. He feels square today." Set down the block.

4. While holding the tube in one hand, pick up each of the small squares one at a time, show them to the audience, then set them down on the tray.

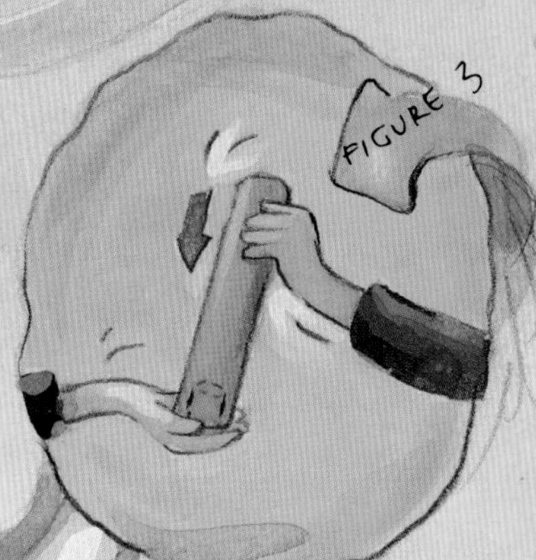

5. Place the bottom of the tube in your opposite palm and lightly grasp the tube (figure 3). As soon as you've grasped the tube, release your grip on the hidden block. Let the block silently slide to the opposite hand.

6. Grip the block while holding the tube upright. Then set the tube on a wooden square. One at a time, put the three blocks into the tube: the two unpainted blocks first, then the blue block.

FIGURE 1

FIGURE 2

FIGURE 3

FIGURE 4

FIGURE 5

7. Announce, "The only problem with working with a ghost is that you can't see when it changes its mind." Lightly squeeze the top block and lift the tube to show the three blocks (figure 4). The audience will see the blue block on the bottom of the stack. Hold the tube at an angle so the audience will see the "empty" tube.

8. Slide the tube over the stack of blocks. Place the second square on top of the tube. Grasping each square, pick up the hidden blocks and slowly turn the stack upside down.

9. Say, "Maybe the ghost will listen to me this time. Blau geist, please demonstrate how you can move through solid matter!" Gripping the top block, remove the tube to show the three blocks with the blue block on the bottom of the stack. Now say, "Well, it did pay attention. It went from top to bottom."

10. Say, "Maybe my ghost has learned some manners!" Separate the stack of three blocks. Put one of the unpainted blocks on a wood square and cover it with the tube while holding the blue block. Pick up the second unpainted block and put it in the top of the tube. As soon as you feel the top blocks touch, stop squeezing the tube so both blocks fall together making one sound. Unknown to your audience, the tube now has a blue block between the two unpainted blocks.

11. Pick up the tube (holding the hidden blue block) to reveal the stack of three blocks. Ta dah! There's the blue ghost in the middle of the stack . Set down the tube on a wooden square. Be sure you turn the tube, so the hidden block doesn't fall noisily onto the square.

12. Arrange the three blocks on the table. While you say, "Please watch as I put the blue ghost into my pocket," pick up the blue block and walk away from the table. As you put your hand with the block into your pocket, slip the block into your jacket sleeve or a hidden pocket in your robe sleeve (see figure 5). You can do this while your hand is hidden deep in your pocket. Once the block is hidden in your sleeve, pull your hand partially out of the pocket so the audience can see your fingers. Hold the pocket open with your opposite hand and pretend to "push" the blue block into the pocket. If you wear a jacket, the sleeve must be tight enough to hold the hidden block. If it feels like the block will slip out, hold your arm close to your body.

13. Remove your hand, showing the audience that it's empty. Say, "I will now encourage the ghost to move again." Walk back to the table. Pick up the tube that contains the hidden block, turning it so the hidden block is on top. Set an unpainted block on a wooden square and slip the tube over it. Now use your free hand to pick up the other unpainted block and put the block into the top of the tube. When the unpainted block touches the hidden, blue block, let them fall together so they make one sound. Shout *Levitatus Repitatus*, Blau Geist!" Remove the tube. The blue block has magically moved from pocket to table!

ABRACA DABRA

FIGURE 5

Magical Cutting of the Cards

PROCEED WITH
CAUTION!

No, this trick is not about a game of wizard poker or dragon hearts. Imagine the astonishment of your viewers as you announce your intention to put your hand through a business card or, better yet, to put your whole body through a playing card. The secret? Skillful scissor work!

WHAT YOU NEED

- business card and deck of playing cards*
- scissors or craft knife
- templates on this page
- adult wizard (optional)

*You'll need to reserve a deck of cards just for this trick.

INSTRUCTIONS

1. Ask for an audience member to donate a business card or to select a card from the deck of cards.

2. Fold the card in half lengthwise.

3. Make cuts through the double thickness alternately from each side, as shown in the template. If you're working with the craft knife, use the ruler to guide the knife, and mind your fingers. Better yet, get an adult wizard to help you.

4. Open up the card. Cut lengthwise through the fold from the first cut to the last.

5. Gently pull the ends to spread apart the cuts. Put your hand or body through the card.

THIS IS THE SIZE OF MOST BUSINESS CARDS, SEE THE TEMPLATES FOR CUTTING ON PAGE 140.

Seeing Is NOT Believing!
The Ghostly Goblet, the Bowl of Invisible Fish, & The Shape-Shifter Puzzle

If you've learned anything by now from your wizard studies, it's that things are often not what they seem. But some mortals can be very stubborn about believing only what their eyes tell them. (How dull!) Here are two amusing optical illusions for you to demonstrate how wrong they can be.

The Ghostly Goblet & the Bowl of Invisible Fish

PROCEED WITH CAUTION!

Here's how to produce a Ghostly Goblet or a Bowl of Invisible Fish out of thin air. The only catch is that you have to be a ghost yourself to use them! But it's fun to make them appear.

WHAT YOU NEED

- helpful adult wizard
- long, thin metal pins, such as beading head pins* or corsage pins**
- wire cutters
- needle-nose pliers
- 1 piece of thin, dark elastic cord 16-inch (40.6 cm)
- pinpoint flashlight (if not available, tape black construction paper over a regular flashlight and poke a small hole through the middle)
- room that can be darkened

*available at beading department of craft stores

**available at florists

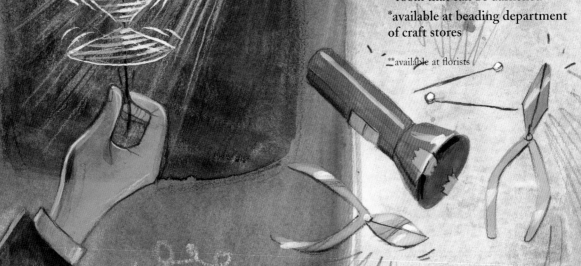

65

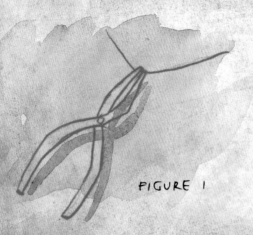

FOR TEMPLATES FOR THE GHOSTLY GOBLET OR THE BOWL OF INVISIBLE FISH, SEE PAGE 140.

FIGURE 1

INSTRUCTIONS

1. If you're working with a pin with a head, such as a corsage pin, ask the adult wizard to use the wire cutters to remove the head.

2. Refer to figure 1. Use the needle-nose pliers to bend the pin into the shape that will produce the desired effect, whether to create a goblet or a fishbowl. Careful, don't stick yourself!

3. Poke the pin through the midpoint of the elastic cord. Practice twisting both ends of the elastic between the thumb and forefinger of both hands, then holding up the cord and drawing the ends apart. The cord should revolve very rapidly, spinning the pin.

4. If the spinning motion causes the pin to flatten so it's perpendicular to the cord, use fine thread to tie one end of the pin to the cord so it remains upright.

5. When you're ready to create the spectral vessel, darken the room and ask a member of the audience to train the flashlight beam on the midpoint of the cord when you hold it up. Twist the elastic, hold up the cord, and pull the ends. The revolving pin will form a brilliantly illuminated shape of the goblet or bowl.

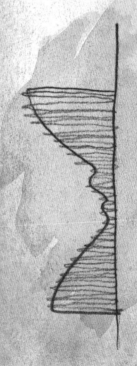

The Shape-Shifter Puzzle

This trick will flummox any dullards who insist on believing only what they can see, when the pieces of this puzzle appear to shrink and expand.

WHAT YOU NEED

• 1 piece of heavy cardboard or poster board, in any rich color (or paint it yourself)
• gold acrylic paint (optional)
• paintbrush (optional)
• magical patterns on page 141 (optional)
• compass
• ruler
• gold gel pen
• pencil
• scissors

INSTRUCTIONS

1. Paint the cardboard, if desired, and let dry. Use the gold acrylic paint to add magical patterns, if you wish.

2. Make a ring on the cardboard by using the compass to draw two concentric circles. Use the ruler and pencil to divide the ring into six equal parts.

3. Using the gold gel pen, trace over the circles and sections. Use the scissors to cut out two sections of the ring.

4. To prepare to show the illusion, place the two sections of the ring on a table, as shown above. Keep the rest of the ring hidden.

5. Ask one of your friends to guess how much longer one piece is than the other. (She will definitely think one is much longer.) Reverse the position of the two sections, and pose the same question to her. Hmm, something strange is going on.

6. Now produce the painted cardboard ring with the two cutouts, and show how the pieces have magically shrunk and expanded to fit!

Sucre Bleu's After Dinner Entertainment

Sucre Bleu, the French wizard and chef to royalty, taught me this trick a few centuries ago. He liked to perform this trick at the end of a meal before the dessert course—using his famous homemade confections. King Louis the Sixteenth loved his bonbons, but the Queen preferred cake. Here's how to change confetti to candy for your own audience.

WHAT YOU NEED

• tall drinking glass with straight parallel sides
• cardboard carton, 10 x 10 x 14 inches (25.4 x 25.4 x 35.6 cm)
• 1 sheet white foam core board
• white or colored tape
• 1 sheet of colored poster board
• small white envelope, about 2 inches (5 cm) square
• cellophane tape
• white craft glue
• rubber cement or spray adhesive (optional)
• rubber bands
• scissors
• craft knife
• pencil
• ruler
• magical patterns on page 141 (optional)
• decorating materials (optional)
• 2 bags of colorful confetti *
• small, individually wrapped hard candies

*You can purchase confetti from craft or party supply stores.

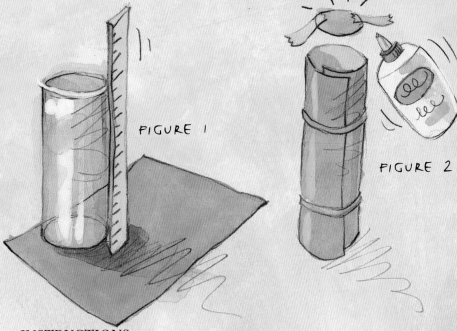

FIGURE 1

FIGURE 2

INSTRUCTIONS

1. Measure the height of your drinking glass. Measure and mark the colored poster board to this height, plus $^1/_8$ inch (3mm). Cut it out (figure 1).

2. Roll the poster board into a cylinder. The cylinder should fit loosely inside the glass. Mark where the end of the poster board overlaps. Remove the cylinder, trim one end as needed approximately 1 inch (2.5 cm) beyond the mark. Overlap the end and glue it to the cylinder. Secure it with rubber bands and let it dry.

3. Place the top of the drinking glass on the poster board. Trace around the outside rim of the glass. Cut out the circle. Spread a white craft glue on the top edge of the cylinder. Turn the cylinder over and center it on the circle. Let it dry. Use a little cellophane tape to secure the circle to the cylinder if needed (figure 2).

4. Spread the confetti in the box. Coat the cylinder with rubber cement or spray adhesive and roll it in the confetti until it is completely covered. Let it dry. This is your "confetti fake."

5. Slip the cylinder into the glass. It should fit easily with the top barely sticking out all around the rim. If the cylinder is a bit too tall, use the scissors to trim a little off the bottom. It should appear to your audience as if the glass is filled with confetti.

6. Make a second tube of poster board about three inches (7.6 cm) taller than the glass. It should fit loosely around the glass. Trim and glue it as you did in step 2, securing it with rubber bands until it is dry (figure 3).

7. Make a small folding screen with two squares of foam core board. Measure and mark the squares 3 inches (7.6 cm) taller than the glass. Cut them out with the craft knife. Set them aside.

8. Cut the flap from the small envelope. Glue the envelope near the top edge of one of the foam core squares.

9. Make a hinge using a length of tape slightly longer than a side of the foam core square. Lay the tape on a flat surface. Place the square without the envelope on the left, and the envelope side on the right. Secure the tape. You may wish to run a second length of tape on the other side of the hinge (figure 4).

10. If desired you may decorate both sides of the screen with any of the magical patterns on page 141 (figure 5).

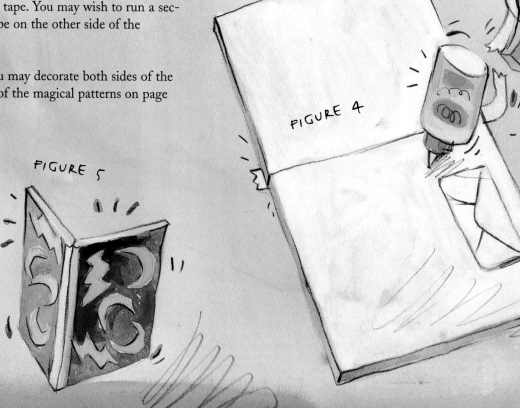

FIGURE 3

FIGURE 4

FIGURE 5

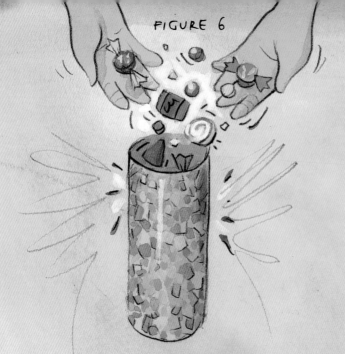

FIGURE 6

FIGURE 7

THE TRICK:
Changing Confetti to Candy

1. Fill the confetti fake with wrapped hard candies. Place the fake—open end up—inside the box (figure 6).

2. Fill the box halfway with confetti. Be very careful not to get any confetti inside the fake with the candy (figure 7).

3. Fill the envelope on the screen with confetti.

4. Place the box with the confetti fake and confetti farther away from the audience on your table. The folded screen (laid flat), poster board tube, and the glass should be closer to the audience.

5. Pick up the glass and pass it to the members of your audience to examine. When you receive the glass again, dip it into the box and scoop out as much confetti as it will hold. Hold the glass above the box and pour out the confetti (figure 8). Take care that you don't pour the confetti into the candy-filled confetti fake.

FIGURE 8

6. Dip the glass back into the box as if you are going to fill it again. This time push the glass down over the fake. When the fake is in the glass, continue to make a scooping motion as you did before. Set the glass–with the fake inside–on the table in front of the box (figure 9).

7. Pick up the poster board tube. Show your audience that it is empty by passing it around or peering through it. Place the tube over the glass.

8. Pick up the screen and open it. Make sure your fingers cover the envelope completely (figure 10). Show both sides of the screen to your audience. Then place the opened screen in front of the covered glass with the envelope side facing you.

9. Move so that the table is just to your left. Grasp the tube with your left hand just about at the rim of the glass. Squeeze the tube slightly. You should be able to feel the confetti fake (figure 11).

10. Pick up the tube and the fake from the glass. Move the tube back over to the box.

11. Misdirect the audience by drawing attention to your right hand. Lower the right hand behind the screen, and take a pinch of confetti from the envelope. This will appear to the audience as if you are picking up confetti from the top of the glass.

12. As you pick up the confetti, lower the tube in your left hand into the box. When the bottom of the tube is slightly below the edge of the box, release the fake and let it slide out of the tube and into the box.

13. Peer through the empty tube at the audience. Place it back over the glass behind the screen.

FIGURE 9

FIGURE 10

FIGURE 11

FIGURE 12

14. Pick up the screen (be sure you cover the envelope with your fingers) and show both sides to the audience. Fold it and lay it down on the table.

15. Lift the tube off the glass. *Voilà!* The candy has magically appeared in the glass (figure 12). Be a good host and pass the candy around for the audience to enjoy.

Edgar Allen Poe, the Chess-Playing Turk, & Other Fabulous Automata

Many fine magicians over the centuries began as scientists—not just alchemists or astronomers, but the kind we call tinkerers. Tinkerers have a gift for experimenting with mechanical things. I especially admired the amazing inventions called automata, mechanical devices that moved on their own. I remember what a sensation the first ones caused several hundred years ago. People were certain they were seeing magic. The most famous automaton was built by Baron von Kempelen, who was the Counsellor of Mechanics to the Empress of Hungary. That's a long way of saying he had an excellent background in tinkering. He named his invention The Chess Playing Turk because, well, obviously, it played chess.

People traveled from all over the world to play the Turk. Napoleon Bonaparte played chess with it a dozen times—and tried to cheat on several occasions! (Each time, the Turk silently corrected the French emperor's illegal moves.) Edgar Allen Poe, student of all things mysterious, saw the Turk and was determined to figure out how it worked. He guessed that there was a person hiding inside

the body, directing the movement of the chess pieces. (He was right about one thing; there was an actual person directing the Turk, but he was hidden in the table beneath the Turk, not inside him! Magnets on the underside of the tabletop showed where the Turk's opponent moved his pieces.)

Which brings me to my friend Jean Eugene Robert-Houdin. Before he became a world-famous magician, Jean repaired watches for a living. One day, instead of some books about watches he'd ordered, Jean received volumes of magic tricks. (Hmm. Was it the hand of fate that mixed up the packages or the hand of a certain wizard? I'll never tell.) So Jean started practicing magic tricks and apprenticed himself to another magician, paying for his education by making and fixing automata. His illusions made him so famous that he became known as Robert-Houdin, the King of Conjurors.

Here's one of his biggest secrets: Jean's tricks were always based on scientific principles. He used electricity to perform mind-reading tricks and made the gate to his house automatic. It opened itself and let him know how many people

had arrived and whether they were good friends or strangers! (I admit even I was astonished the first time I walked in and Jean had a plate of my favorite pastries waiting for me.) As wizards and magicians learned over the years, some people reject what they don't understand. That was the case with René Descartes, a studious young fellow from France. He made an automaton named Francine, who moved just like a real person. Unfortunately, René took her on a sea voyage and some of his fellow passengers didn't understand how Francine worked. Not being good scientists, the only explanation they could think of was that Francine was possessed by an evil spirit. They threw her overboard, and René made himself scarce. ("She sink, therefore I ran," he told me.) Descartes never made another automaton and devoted himself to the study of math and philosophy instead. What a loss to the world of magic!

Chapter 5

FLYING, LEVITATION, & ESCAPOLOGY

Floating, flying, making things move, and getting out of impossible bonds are a wizard's stock in trade. So you need to learn how to make balls, rings, and scarves float and dance! (Hint: buy some black thread. See page 76.) I also include one of my favorite little tricks, Escape from the Enchanted Chain (page 86). I learned much of this in Europe, but the New World was full of magic too. Consider the Shaking Tent of the Native American conjuror Was-chus-co. Tied up head to toe, he was left alone in a tent. The tent began to shake and animal voices and howls issued. Then all became quiet. People peeked inside to find him sitting peacefully on the pile of ropes, free as a bird.

The Sorcerer's Handkerchief

Any sorcerer worth his spellbook knows how to make his own pocket handkerchief untie itself. You'll want to perform this illusion in a dimly lit room or far enough away from your audience so that its secret remains a mystery known only to you.

WHAT YOU NEED

- silk or nylon scarf, approximately 22 inches (cm) square
- magical patterns on page 141 (optional)
- gold acrylic paint (optional)
- paint brush (optional)
- sewing needle
- fine black thread or very thin fishing line, 3 feet (0.9 m) long

INSTRUCTIONS

1. If desired, decorate the scarf with painted designs.

2. Some magicians separate the strands of a thread to make it finer and harder to see. Experiment to see how fine you can make the thread while keeping it strong enough to do the trick. Thread the needle. Using several small stitches, attach one end of the thread to a corner of the scarf.

3. After removing the needle, make a knot at the free end of the thread.

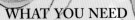

FIGURE 1

FIGURE 2

The Illusion

Making the Scarf Untie Itself

1. Stand against a dark background in a dimly lit room. Hold the scarf by the corners and demonstrate to your audience that there's nothing hidden on either side.

2. While using one hand to hold the threaded corner of the scarf, use the other hand to grab the corner that's diagonally opposite. Still holding both corners, twirl the scarf until it's wrapped around itself.

3. Here's the part you need to have practiced a lot. Tie a loose knot in the center of the wrapped scarf, making sure the loose end of the thread runs through the knot (figure 1).

4. Holding one end of the scarf so its threaded end points to the floor, very casually move one of your feet, trapping the knotted end of the thread between your foot and the floor (figure 2).

5. Command, *"Houdinius Assistas!"* and slowly raise your hand which holds the scarf. The thread will pull the corner of the scarf, and the audience will see the scarf untie itself.

The Mysterious Celestial Sphere

The French conjurer Robert-Houdin was famous for levitating a golden globe on stage. Just for fun, he also used to do it with crumpled menus in restaurants in Paris. The waiter would take one look, drop his tray, and fly out the door! (I learned to eat fast when Robert was around.) Anyway, in this illusion you'll hold a balled-up piece of metal foil in your open palm. As you apply spells with the other hand, the ball will rise. Your audience will be truly agog when you pass your hands around the floating ball, pluck it out of the air, and throw it at them! Perform this illusion in a dimly lit room.

WHAT YOU NEED

- roll of aluminum foil
- scissors
- spool of fine black thread
- chair with a slatted back or another style to which you can tie a thread

INSTRUCTIONS

1. Use the scissors to cut off a 4-foot (1.2 m) piece of thread. As shown in figure 1, tie one end to the top of the chair back. Tie a loop that's big enough to fit over your right ear in the other end. Adjust the length of the string, if necessary, cutting a new piece to fit your height and the chair's height.

2. Put the roll of aluminum foil on the chair, and position the chair to the right of where you'll stand while performing.

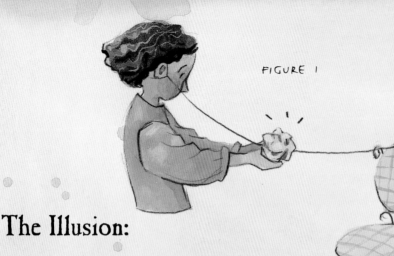

FIGURE 1

The Illusion:

Making the Sphere Rise

1. When you're ready to perform, slip the thread loop over your right ear.

2. Pick up the aluminum foil and tear off a 12-inch-square (30.5 cm) piece. Turn toward your right, and put one foot slightly in front of the other. Set the roll of foil on the chair seat.

3. Still standing in position, extend your arms and use both hands to crumple the piece of foil. Shape it around the thread that runs from your ear to the the chair (figure 1), discreetly making sure the ball can move freely on the thread.

4. Extending your right hand, hold the ball on your open palm and back away from the chair, slowly putting your weight on your rear foot. The thread will start to grow tighter. Pronounce magical commands and wave your left hand over the ball, which rises as the slack in the string is taken up (figure 2).

5. Keeping your head very still, wave both hands around the floating ball, but be careful not to touch the thread. Galloping gargoyles, it floats (as far as the audience is concerned)!

6. Position your left hand under the ball. Slowly shift your weight to your front foot, slackening the thread so the ball sinks into your palm.

7. Without pausing, turn to face your audience, and walk toward them with your hand extended, the ball in it. The thread should slip through the foil and fall unseen to the floor. Throw the ball to someone in the audience, and see if he'll catch it or if he's too spooked!

FIGURE 2

Flying Card and Coin

Every wizard knows how to make objects fly, and you're no exception. This trick is fun and simple to do. You're certain to win if your friends bet you it can't be done. (Don't let them know how long you've been practicing.)

WHAT YOU NEED

- a penny
- a playing card

INSTRUCTIONS

1. Balance the playing card on the tip of the index finger of your left hand.

2. Place the penny on top of the card, centering it over the fingertip.

3. Flick the edge of the card sharply, using the forefinger and thumb of your right hand. The card will fly off while the penny stays on your finger.

Freya's Floating Ring

You may already know about Freya's golden necklace, which shone as brilliantly as the stars. She was one Norse goddess who definitely liked jewelry, and I wouldn't put it past her to use her powers to borrow a mortal's bauble. One heaven-sent Levitation Spell and, Zap! It was hers. That's why sometimes after you lose a trinket, it shows up again where you'd swear you already looked. In this illusion, you'll use your Never-Fail Magic Wand (page 18) and a secret thread to make a ring move up and down all by itself.

INSTRUCTIONS

1. Remove one end cap from the wand. Tie one end of the thread to the wand's end, and slip the cap back over it.

2. Wear the shirt or belt under your robe. Tie the other end of the thread onto a button or the belt buckle. Stick the wand in a left-hand pocket of your robe. Hide the ring in another pocket.

3. To start the performance, tell your audience the story of Freya. Ask someone to loan you a ring. (If no one has one, take the spare one from your pocket.) Walking back to your performance area (not too close to the audience), say, "This is a very nice ring. Hmm, I'd swear I felt it jump! I wonder if Freya has spotted it?"

4. Use your left hand to take the wand out of your pocket, holding it so the end attached to the thread

WHAT YOU NEED

• 1 length of black thread, 18 inches (45.7 cm) long
• Never-Fail Magic Wand (page 18)
• 1 shirt with buttons, or a belt with buckle
• 1 ring, in a size that slides easily over the wand

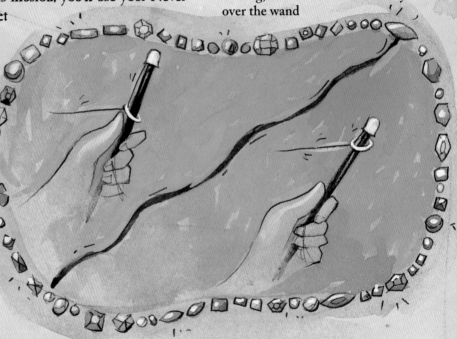

points up. With your right hand, slip the ring down the wand over the thread and down the wand to the point where it reaches your left fingers (figure 1).

5. Say, "I don't blame Freya for wanting this ring. Let's see if she left any magic sprinkled on it." Keeping your left hand and the wand still, gesture with your right hand and move your body backward

as you say, "Rise, I command you!" The ring will now rise (figure 2). Then say, "That's far enough. Sink, I say," gesturing with your right hand and moving your body forward so the ring sinks. Repeat a few times. You can even freeze the ring at mid-wand for a moment and say,

"FREYA! LET GO!"

6. Remove the ring and give it back to the owner, saying, "Watch out. She may decide she wants it!"

Tubus Newtonius

Much of early magic was based on scientific principles. You've heard how Sir Isaac Newton came up with the idea of gravity while he rested under an apple tree in the delightful English countryside. At this point, the stories differ. Either he observed a falling apple or one bonked him on the head. Actually, both versions are correct. When I saw Sir Isaac roll over to resume his nap after the first apple fell, I adjusted the aim of my Descending Charm and scored a direct hit with the next one. (Sometimes we wizards have to help scientific progress.) In this illusion, you'll use magic to make tubes defy gravity.

WHAT YOU NEED

- 2 cardboard tubes
- magical patterns and decorating materials on pages 138 and 141 (optional)
- brightly colored wrapping or construction paper
- pencil
- ruler
- scissors
- glue stick or spray adhesive
- rubber bands
- awl or large needle
- 1 strip of construction paper or poster board, $1/2$ x 8-inch (1.3 x 20.3 cm)
- 3 lengths of string, each 3 feet (0.9 m) long
- cellophane tape
- 1 small plastic curtain ring, $1/2$ inch (1.3 cm) in diameter

INSTRUCTIONS

1. You'll need to decorate each tube to impress your audience. Choose a patterned wrapping paper, or draw magical patterns onto plain construction paper.

2. Lay one of the tubes on the paper, lining up one edge of the tube with your paper's edge. Mark the top edge of the tube on the paper. Roll the tube a little way and make another mark. Join the marks with the pencil and extend the line, using the ruler to make a straight line (figure 1).

3. Cut out the paper along the line.

4. Wrap the paper around the tube. Mark just beyond where it overlaps itself. Unroll the paper, make a straight line at the mark with the ruler and pencil. Cut along the line.

5. Use the glue stick or spray adhesive to adhere the paper to each tube. Work carefully to avoid wrinkles. Use the rubber bands to secure the paper to the tube (figure 2). Let dry.

6. Using the awl or needle, make a small hole about $\frac{1}{2}$ inch (1.3 cm) from each end of the $\frac{1}{2}$-inch-wide (1.3 cm) strip of paper (figure 3).

7. Run one of the strings through each hole. Move the paper to the center of the string.

8. Place 1-inch (2.5 cm) strips of cellophane tape between the string and the paper. Slip the paper and string into the center of the tube. Press the paper and tape against the side of the tube. Make sure the string moves freely through the tube (figure 4). This is tube number one.

9. Tape an end of another piece of string to the inside of the second tube, near one end of the tube.

10. Tie the third piece of string securely to the small curtain ring. Lower the ring through the tube, and thread the opposite string through the ring (figure 5). This is tube number two.

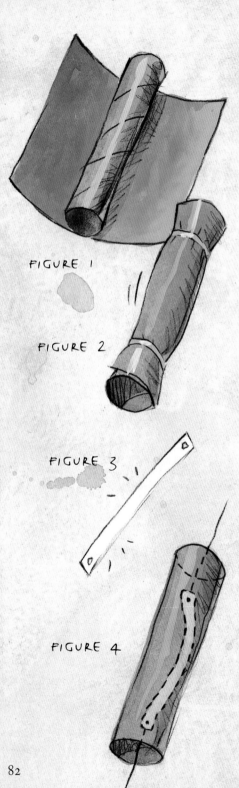

FIGURE 1

FIGURE 2

FIGURE 3

FIGURE 4

FIGURE 5

The Illusion:

Making the Tubes Rise

1. Pick up tube number one. Pull gently on each end of the string (figure 3) to keep it taut. (Practice how to do this discreetly.) Tell Newton's story and announce that this tube has the ability to resist the law of gravity at your command.

2. Slightly relax the tension of the string and the tube will begin to slip down. Shout, "*Gravitas Desistas!*" and gently tighten the string. The tube will stop moving. Set the tube down.

3. Pick up tube number two. Hold both ends of the string; the audience will think it's one string. The top string holds up the tube. Gently pull on the bottom string to keep the tube in what appears to be the center of the string. This becomes easier with practice.

4. Say, "This tube will now reverse gravity. *Gravitas Resistas!*" If you gently pull on the top string, the tube will appear to rise!

The Melting (Not) Knot

Many people thought that escape artist Harry Houdini must be a genuine sorcerer. How else could he escape time after time from ropes and knots and handcuffs? Maybe he just used the power of his mind to unfasten them. (Guess who taught him.) Your friends will react the same way when they watch you make a knot in your handkerchief, then watch you unknot it without touching it!

WHAT YOU NEED

• 1 plain white handkerchief or Thin Air Scarf (page 35)

INSTRUCTIONS

1. Twirl the handkerchief so it forms a coiled "rope." Hold it between the middle and index fingers of each hand (figure 1).

2. Take the end held by your right hand and lay it between your left thumb and forefinger (figure 2), continuing to hold part of the handkerchief with your right hand.

3. Position part of the handkerchief (the part still held by the right hand) between the second and third fingers of the left hand, while at the same time you use your right hand to reach

FIGURE 1

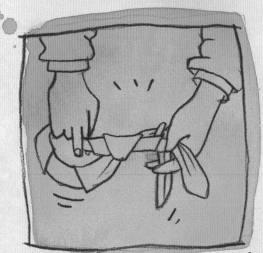

FIGURE 2

through the loop and grab
the closest dangling end (figure 3).

4. Pull the end through the loop
while keeping your grip on the part
of the handkerchief that's between
the second and third fingers of the
left hand (figure 4). A loop will form
around your middle left finger.

FIGURE 3

5. Casually withdraw the
finger while keeping the
loop hidden behind the
knot, and show your friends
the knot while holding it, as
shown in figure 5.

6. Blow on the knot, shaking
it slightly. Watch it melt
away!

FIGURE 4

FIGURE 5

Escape from the Enchanted Chain

There's never been a man-made rope or chain so strong that it could defeat a properly trained wizard—unless it was fortified by a proper Hold-All Spell or Disarm Charm. In this illusion, you'll create a chain in front of your friends' eyes, then magically break it apart. It's most effective when performed close-up for a few people.

WHAT YOU NEED

• two plastic drinking straws*

*You'll want to have extras to practice with.

INSTRUCTIONS

1. Needless to say, study the illustrations closely and practice this trick until you have memorized it flawlessly. (Just as you do with your homework, right?)

2. Lay one straw on top of and at right angles to the other (figure 1). Bend the vertical straw down and under the horizontal stem (figure 2), then up (figure 3).

3. Grasp the right end of the horizontal straw. Twist it under the left end of the horizontal straw and under the top end of the vertical straw (figure 4).

4. Bring the left end of the horizontal straw to the right (figure 5).

5. Manipulating the vertical straw, bring the top end down and the bottom end up so they "meet" on the left (figure 6). Your chain should now look like figure 7.

6. Grasp the ends and pull (figures 8 and 9). Let go of one end of each straw so they pop up. Aha! Your magic has worked once again, and the chain has magically separated.

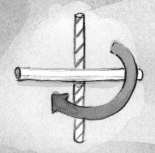

FIGURE 1

FIGURE 2

FIGURE 3

FIGURE 4

FIGURE 5

FIGURE 6

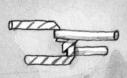

FIGURE 7

FIGURE 8

FIGURE 9

Merlin's Enchanted Spell Book

PROCEED WITH CAUTION!

I used to entertain my apprentices with a version of this trick when they began their levitation lessons. They caught on quickly and soon cards, photos, and homework were rising up and sailing out of the classroom. I named this piece of magic in honor of my friend Merlin. Legend says that after 15,000 soldiers failed to move some giant boulders so much as a hair, Merlin made them float up from the earth and set them gently in boats. After crossing the Irish Channel to England, he floated the stones to a place where they still stand, called Stonehenge. Now, THAT'S levitation!

SHOW STOPPER

FIGURE 1

FIGURE 2

FIGURE 3

WHAT YOU NEED

• large hardback book*
• magical patterns and decorating materials on page 138 and 141 (optional)
• pencil
• ruler
• sharp awl
• drill and fine drill bit (optional)
• helpful adult wizard (optional)
• spool of fine black thread
• sewing needle
• cellophane tape

*Purchase a used book from a thrift store for this trick.

INSTRUCTIONS

1. Discard the book jacket if the book has one.

2. Add magical patterns of your choice to the front and back covers of the book. (A glittery, fancy-looking book will say, "MAGIC!" to your audience.) You might also write a new title on the cover. Let any wet decorations dry before proceeding (figure 1).

3. On the first inside page of the book, make a mark $3/4$ inch (1.9 cm) down from the top edge and 2 inches (5 cm) in from the side.

4. With the adult wizard's help, use the awl or drill to pierce through all of the pages and the back cover. If you are using an awl, you will have to pierce through a few pages, mark a later page, and continue to pierce sev-

eral pages at a time. A drill is a much faster way to pierce through the pages. Just get an adult wizard to help you and be sure you use the smallest drill bit you can find (figure 2).

5. Measure and cut off a 4-foot (1.2 m) length of black thread. Thread it through the eye of the needle.

6. Starting from the front of the book, thread the needle through the pierced pages and back cover. Leave a 6-inch (15.2 cm) tail hanging from the first page (figure 3).

7. Tape the thread tail securely to the inside front cover of the book.

8. Tie a small loop in the other end of the thread. Allow most of the thread to hang behind the back cover.

The Illusion:

Levitating Cards from
Merlin's Spell Book

FIGURE 4

WHAT YOU NEED

- deck of playing cards
- Merlin's Spell Book
- waist-high table,
  or Magician's Stage Table (page 19)
- helpful assistant (optional)

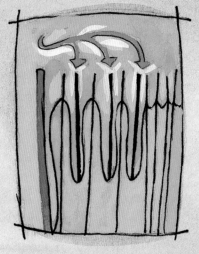

FIGURE 5

INSTRUCTIONS

1. Backstage, slip the thread loop around a button on your clothing at waist or chest level. Place the deck of cards in one of your pockets. Now make your entrance carrying the book in front of you with both hands. Make sure its front cover faces outward (figure 4).

2. Standing behind the table, place the book upright on the tabletop. The front cover faces the audience. While you're telling them the story about Merlin, remove the deck of cards from your pocket and set them on the table in front of the book. Take care to position yourself in such a way that the thread is not easily seen by the audience.

3. Have your assistant carry the deck of cards into the audience and have someone choose three cards from the deck. Or have a volunteer come to the table, turn his back to you, and select three cards from the deck and place them on the table before returning to his seat.

4. This next step demands the most practice; repeat it until you can slip each card into the book without revealing the thread. It can be done! While you say, "You know, I've used this deck of cards for a long time," pick up the book with one hand, holding it closed. Use your opposite hand to pick up each card one at a time. Move from the front to the

back of the book, slipping each card between the pages and pushing it down (figure 5). Each card will catch the thread. You'll see and feel the length of thread at the back of the book grow shorter as you do this, and you may need to subtly move the book toward your body.

5. When all the cards are hidden in the book, place your free hand above the book and say, "Let's see if any magic rubbed off." Move your hand in a circular motion above the book and intone, *"Merlinus Assistus! Chartas Flotatus!"* At the same time, use your other hand to gently move the book away from your body just enough to make the cards mysteriously rise.

Harry Houdini, Master Escape Artist

You might say that the first thing Harry Houdini ever escaped was his name. Born Ehrich Weiss, he changed his name to Houdini in honor of his favorite magician, Robert-Houdin, the great French maker of automata. Houdini also changed his little brother's name, and they set up rival acts to attract publicity. (Little brothers do come in handy sometimes!)

Houdini specialized in escaping from dangerous situations, such as the time he was put in a straight jacket and hung upside down from a crane in California. Trunks, ropes, shackles, handcuffs, leg irons—he escaped them all. What led him to master this life-threatening form of magic? Harry used to say that it was better than making neckties, his first job. But one night after a show, Harry told me that he actually became an escape artist in order to get out of situations he'd put himself into.

You see, Houdini liked to (loudly) denounce anyone who practiced any sort of supernatural art. In fact, he challenged people to perform supernatural feats on stage and later showed the audience how to reproduce these feats using mechanical means. Now, giving away professional secrets is not only rude, it can be downright dangerous. Here's an inside story only a few wizards know.

Houdini once challenged Theophrastus Bombastus, a real wizard masquerading as a stage conjuror. Houdini managed to duplicate the wizard's illusion, and Theo lost his temper and teleported Houdini to a Swiss dairy. To be more specific, Harry found himself inside a big milk tank! Luckily, dairy maids heard Houdini banging on the tank and let him out. After that, Houdini studied the art of escapology with a vengeance. So now you know what really inspired one of Houdini's favorite stage tricks, the Milk Can Escape.

Houdini made sure he could pull off every trick, and he never got cocky about his own abilities. He also always had an assistant standing nearby to rescue him at the first sign of trouble. Despite these precautions, Harry almost got killed a few times. So don't even THINK about copying any of Houdini's illusions, young wizard, or I'll turn you into a top hat and you'll spend the rest of your life coping with bird feathers and rabbit's breath. Ever *smelled* rabbit's breath?

Anyway, Houdini could hold his breath an amazingly long time, and his favorite trick was the Water Torture Cell. (I thought it was quite terrifying.) He was bound in chains and lowered head first into a chamber filled with water. His ankles were locked and bound into the lid of the cell, and the lid secured in the cell.

Houdini hung upside down for a few moments, keeping everyone in suspense. Could he escape before he drowned? An assistant drew a curtain across the cell. As the orchestra played eerie music, Houdini wriggled and wiggled and twisted and bent until the chains fell off, then hoisted himself up to the top of the cell where a bit of air was trapped. He took a deep breath, picked the locks around his ankles, then slid the trick lid off the cell. He appeared, drenched but unharmed, in front of the curtain. Tah dah! All at once, spectators gasped and started to breathe again themselves.

Audience members then inspected the cell. There it stood, still locked, with a giant pile of chains at the bottom of the tank. Harry went on to astonish audiences for years to come, until he passed away on—you guessed it—Halloween.

Chapter 6

LiTTLE TiNy PieCes

I vividly remember when the Great Wizard of the North performed for Queen Victoria at Balmoral, her castle in Scotland. Would you believe he had the nerve to borrow her handkerchief and cut it into pieces?! Wisely, he restored it to one piece and returned it with a bow to its owner. Otherwise, the royal We would not have been amused. This chapter includes some of my best rope tricks, including the Rope that Can't Be Cut (page 94). Or try your skills at Sawing a Matchbook in Half—with a playing card! (page 99). For a real showstopper, I also share the secret of how to pass solid rings through ropes in the Magic Rings and Ropes Extravaganza (page 101).

The Rope that Can't Be Cut

Your ordinary stage magician's usual objective is to escape from ropes, chains, handcuffs, steamer trunks, laundry bags, and whatnot. But I think it's much more wizardly to demonstrate (*Separatus reversus!*) how we can put things back together that were broken or whacked in half.

WHAT YOU NEED

• scissors
• lightweight, white string, one 2 feet (61 cm) long and one 3 inches (7.6 cm) long
• helpful adult wizard
• paraffin wax*
• clean, empty tin can

*available in the canning supplies section of a grocery store

94

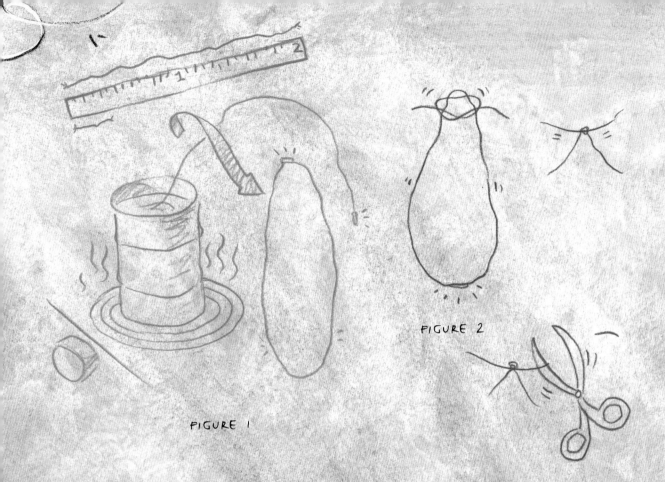

FIGURE 1

FIGURE 2

INSTRUCTIONS

1. Use the scissors to cut one 2-foot (61 cm) piece of string and a 3-inch (7.6 cm) piece. It's a good idea to cut extras to use for practice.

2. With an adult wizard's help, put the paraffin in the tin can and follow the directions on the packaging to melt it on a stovetop.

3. While the paraffin is in liquid form, dip $1/2$ inch (1.3 cm) of each end of the string into the wax. When the wax cools and starts to turn white, roll the two ends of the string together between your fingers to form an invisible join as the wax hardens (figure 1). Let cool completely.

4. Refer to figure 2. At the point of the circle opposite the wax join, squeeze the string together. Using the 3-inch (7.6 cm) piece of string, tie a simple overhand knot over the doubled strings. Carefully pull the protruding string of the joined circle almost all the way through the knot, leaving a tiny part inside the knot. The key is to tie the knot tightly

enough that it won't fall off when you display the string in step 6 but loosely enough so you can pull it off in step 3 of the illusion on page 96.

5. Use the scissors to trim the ends of the fake knot, leaving $3/4$-inch-long (1.9 cm) tails on each side of the knot.

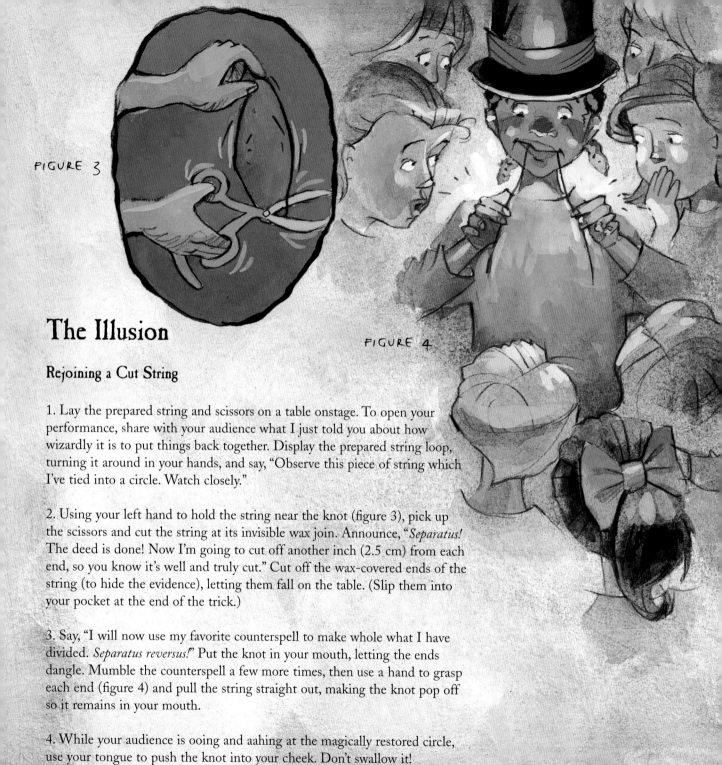

FIGURE 3

FIGURE 4

The Illusion

Rejoining a Cut String

1. Lay the prepared string and scissors on a table onstage. To open your performance, share with your audience what I just told you about how wizardly it is to put things back together. Display the prepared string loop, turning it around in your hands, and say, "Observe this piece of string which I've tied into a circle. Watch closely."

2. Using your left hand to hold the string near the knot (figure 3), pick up the scissors and cut the string at its invisible wax join. Announce, "*Separatus! The deed is done!* Now I'm going to cut off another inch (2.5 cm) from each end, so you know it's well and truly cut." Cut off the wax-covered ends of the string (to hide the evidence), letting them fall on the table. (Slip them into your pocket at the end of the trick.)

3. Say, "I will now use my favorite counterspell to make whole what I have divided. *Separatus reversus!*" Put the knot in your mouth, letting the ends dangle. Mumble the counterspell a few more times, then use a hand to grasp each end (figure 4) and pull the string straight out, making the knot pop off so it remains in your mouth.

4. While your audience is ooing and aahing at the magically restored circle, use your tongue to push the knot into your cheek. Don't swallow it!

The Mysterious Tie that Binds

To prepare this astonishing illusion, you'll string playing cards on two pieces of string. But you haven't used just any old string—it has the ability to repair itself after it's been cut in two. Or at least your audience will think so.

WHAT YOU NEED

• 10 playing cards
• ruler
• pencil
• hole punch
• 2 pieces of string, thin cord, or ribbon, each 12 inches (30.5 cm) long
• scissors

INSTRUCTIONS

1. Use the ruler and pencil to make a mark 1 inch (2.5 cm) from each end of a playing card and at an equal distance from each side (figure 1).

2. Punch a hole at each mark, then use the card as a template to punch holes at the same places on the remaining nine cards.

3. With the cards stacked on top of each other, run a string through each set of holes (figure 2).

3. Here's the secret. As shown in figure 3, rotate the cards at the top and bottom of the stack a half-turn to make the strings cross.

4. To perform the illusion, grip the cards tightly in a stack (so the crossed strings are hidden). Displaying them to your audience, move the stack back and forth on the strings so the viewers will conclude the cards are strung together as they seem to be. Tell a story to your audience: "Did you know that wizards often carry backup supplies in case we have a bad day with spell cast-

FIGURE 1

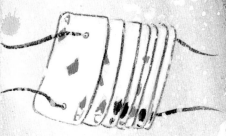

FIGURE 2

FIGURE 3

FIGURE 4

ing? I never leave home without my Magical Self-Mending String. That's what I used to put these cards together. Allow me to demonstrate!"

5. Ask a volunteer from the audience to choose one of the strings to cut. Before letting him make the cut, loosely wrap the two ends of the other piece of string around the end of the stack and hold them in place.

6. Spread the cards apart at the top, untied end (figure 4), and allow the volunteer to use the scissors to cut the exposed string.

7. As you announce, "Now I will activate the Self-Mending String," square up the cards and tap them dramatically. Offer the strand at the top of the deck to the volunteer and direct him to pull "the magically mended string" all the way out. (Loosen your grip on the strings wrapped around the bottom.) He'll pull out an entire, uncut string! (He really pulled out the string that criss-crossed up from the bottom. But that's our secret.)

98

Sawing a Matchbox in Half

PROCEED WITH CAUTION!

Of all the mortal magicians I ever saw, Percy T. Selbit was the best at sawing ladies in half with style, then putting them back together. Being English, he was, of course, extremely polite about it. Other magicians copied his tricks because they were so good, but Percy declined the suggestion that he put a thief in his magic box, cut him in two, and leave him in pieces. I never missed an issue of *The Wizard*, Percy's monthly magazine. I was always interested in seeing what kind of magic nonwizards could create without our help. Here's how to use a simple playing card to saw a matchbox in half, then put it back together again.

WHAT YOU NEED

- deck of cards
- small box of safety matches
- pencil
- metal-edge ruler
- sharp craft knife
- adult wizard
- elastic beading thread
- glue gun and hot glue sticks

INSTRUCTIONS

1. From the deck of cards, select the six, seven, and eight of hearts, diamonds, spades, or clubs. The three cards should all be of the same suit.

2. Center the box of safety matches on one long side of a card. Slide up the end of the box to cover the card's suit mark (the diamond, heart, club, or spade in the middle of the card). Trace around the box.

3. With the help of an adult wizard, use the metal-edge ruler and craft knife to cut out the shape. Trace the shape of the cutout onto a second card and cut it out (figure 1).

FIGURE 1

4. Place the matchbox lengthwise on the long edge of the third card. Slide it up to cover the suit mark in the middle. Trace around the shape. Before you cut out this shape, add an extra $\frac{1}{2}$ inch (1.3 cm) to the height. It should be taller than the spaces you cut out in step 3.

5. Cut two 2-inch (5 cm) lengths of the elastic beading thread. Wrap each length around the piece you cut out in step 4. Knot the ends together. Make sure the elastic beading thread fits tightly.

6. Lay one card face up on a flat surface. Place the two knotted beading threads on either side of the cutout. The knots should be on the bottom edge of the card. Carefully squeeze a tiny amount of hot glue on the knots to secure them to the card.

7. Slip the small cut piece of card into the loops of the elastic beading thread.

8. Lay the second card on top of the elastic thread. Adjust the small cutout to center the suit mark, so the assembly appears to be one card (figure 2).

9. With the adult wizard's help, use hot glue to glue most of the way around the perimeter of the card. You don't want the glue to go beyond the elastic or to touch the small piece of card.

FIGURE 2

The Illusion:

Sawing a Matchbox in Half and Making It Whole Again

1. Slip the prepared card on top of the deck of cards. Then announce to your audience, "For true wizards, it's not necessary to use saws to cut things in half. I will demonstrate the principle by using a simple playing card to cut a matchbox in two."

2. Pick up the prepared card and show both sides to the audience. (Place your fingers on the cut piece to disguise the cut.)

3. Place the matchbox on the table. Command, "*Cartas Divedens!*" [KAR-tuss DIH-vuh-DENS]. Press the cut portion of the card onto the box. Display it to your audience. The card has cut through the box!

4. Now announce, "As wizards, we also have the ability to put things back together again. *Cartas Replicares!*" [KAR-tuss REH-plih-KAH-ress] Remove the card. The box has been magically restored to one piece!

Magic Rings and Ropes Extravaganza

You may send your audience running for the exits, if I told you how to stroll through a solid wall before your spectators' eyes. Better to use some smaller items to demonstrate the principle. This illusion features not one but four magic rings and five scarves that appear to pass through solid rope.

AMAZING!

WHAT YOU NEED

- 4 large, circular embroidery hoops
- gold acrylic paint
- paintbrush
- small plastic jewels (optional)
- white craft glue (optional)
- 2 pieces of clothesline, each 10 feet (3 m) long
- 4- to 6-inch (10.2 to 15.2 cm) piece of monofilament fishing line
- 5 scarves in vibrant colors

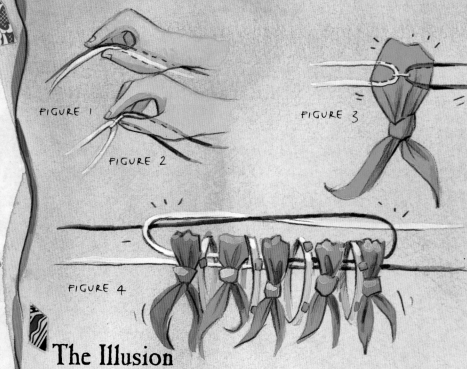

FIGURE 1

FIGURE 2

FIGURE 3

FIGURE 4

INSTRUCTIONS

1. Paint the hoops gold and let dry, then decorate their outer surfaces with glued-on plastic jewels, if desired.

2. Place the two pieces of clothesline side by side. At their midpoint, use the fishing line to tie a snug loop (figure 1). Arrange the rope, hoops, and scarves on a table.

FIGURE 1

The Illusion

Passing Rings and Scarves Through Rope

1. To open your performance, tell your audience that you've found it frightens viewers too much to see you walk through solid objects, and therefore you'll demonstrate your powers another way. Pick up the tied-together clotheslines in the middle, using your hand to cover the fishing line. Have two volunteers from the audience pick up the ends and ask them to pull hard "to see how strong they are." Keep holding the middle while they do this.

2. Now ask the volunteers to let go of the lines. Hand them the hoops and scarves and tell them to examine each one. Say, "They look quite ordinary, right? Can't see any magic in them?" While they're doing this (and the rest of the audience is watching them), use your thumb, and then your thumb and forefinger, to separate and reposition the two pieces of clothesline at the fishing line loop, as shown in figure 2.

3. Keeping your hand over the loop, ask your volunteers to pick up the opposite ends of the clothesline. Tie a scarf at the midpoint to hide the ends of the lines and the fishing line loop (figure 3). Say, "But on the other hand, a wizard only has to wear a thing once to leave a little magic on it."

4. Have the volunteers slide two embroidery hoops onto the lines, one on either side of the scarf. Tie on two more scarves, then slide on two more hoops. Slide the hoops and scarves to the center.

5. While you say, "Okay, let's make sure these are really secure," take the end of one clothesline from each volunteer and double them back toward the center. Tie the ropes over the hoops and scarves, as shown in figure 4, then hand each volunteer the end of a clothesline. (I'll tell you a secret. This reversal of the clotheslines' ends means each volunteer once again holds an end from each rope. The lines in figure 4 are color-coded so you can see what I mean.)

6. Now say, "Are you ready? Get a strong grip and brace yourselves. When I say the magic words '*Herakles Assistus*,' [HAIR-uh-KLEES uh-SISS-tuss] pull as hard as you can! Okay, *Herakles Assistus!*"

7. The fishing line loop will snap and the scarves and hoops will fly free of the rope!

YOU'RE A STAR.

Sawing Ladies   in Half
& Other Fairly Gruesome Illusions

Magicians are always coming up with new ways to dismember, decapitate, and otherwise disassemble their assistants onstage, and then put them back together. It's all clever illusion. And by the way, young wizard, I FORBID you to remove any body parts from any living creature, including your little sister. It's just not done. If you ignore me, I'll turn you into a flatworm and you'll lose your head again and again in biology class!

Now, where was I? The great magician Alexander Hermann used to cut off his assistant's head, set it on a table, and carry on a conversation with it! He then restored it to its owner. (Alexander also liked to switch things on serving platters in fancy restaurants, so when the waiter lifted the silver cover, Surprise!)

The most famous gruesome illusion remains the sawing-a-lady-in-half trick. (And why is it only ladies and not gentlemen, my sister sorceresses grumpily ask? Good question.) Percy T. Selbit and Horace Goldin used to compete with each other when it came to whose sawing-in-half act was the best and most dangerous looks-wise. Selbit's assistants poured buckets of red liquid (Ugh!) in front of theaters. Goldin stationed ambulances, nurses with stretchers, and men dressed as undertakers at the performance. He also ran ads for female participants, guaranteeing "$10,000 in case of fatality!"

So how is it done? The magician's assistant climbs into a large box so her head pokes out one end and her feet the other. The magician tickles her feet to prove they're real, then produces a wicked-looking saw and proceeds to saw the box in half. (Harry Blackstone, Jr., used a giant buzz saw.) When he's finished, the magician separates the two boxes completely. There's only thin air in between his assistant's top half and bottom half! Then he puts the box back together, waves his wand, and out steps the assistant, smiling and unharmed.

But how was it really done? There are two ways to create this illusion. While the magician flourishes his saw to distract the audience, the assistant pulls her legs up to her chest inside the box, above the saw line, and pokes fake legs out the other end. Or a second woman is hidden in a box under the table, which has a false bottom. While the first woman pulls her legs up, the second woman sticks her legs up and out of the box. But to any magician using the second method: Don't forget to signal the top half to start laughing, when you tickle the feet at the bottom!

Chapter 7

FUN AT THE TABLE & IN THE PARLOUR

Magic can happen anywhere, not just onstage. Sometimes illusions are most effective when you create them on a small scale in front of an audience of two or three people. After dinner is good time to conjure up some parlour magic, but if you'd really like to surprise your family, see page 109 to learn how to levitate the salt shaker during a meal. If you want to follow in the footsteps of Nevil Maskelyne, one of the magic world's most skillful plate spinners, try the Floating Banquet Ware trick on page 108. This chapter also contains directions for making a flutter ring, one of my absolute favorite magical gadgets; see the Wizard Post illusion on page 110.

The Fork in the Fork Trick

This illusion is based on a simple form of prestidigitation. You'll use hand movements to control what your audience sees and how they see it, so they'll swear you're actually bending metal by simply stroking it. This trick is best performed for an audience of one one person.

FIGURE 2

FIGURE 1

FIGURE 3

WHAT YOU NEED

- lightweight metal fork
- pliers

INSTRUCTIONS

1. Use the pliers to bend the far left tine of the fork at a 45° angle (figure 1). Slip the fork into your robe pocket or another hiding place.

2. When you're ready to perform, remove the fork from your pocket, keeping your thumb over the bent tine.

3. Raise your right hand, palm down, to eye level. Covering the bent tine with your left thumb and keeping it on the side hidden from your audience, move the fork up and towards your right hand. Use your right thumb and forefinger to grasp the fork handle (figure 2).

4. Rotate the hand holding the fork until it's perpendicular to the floor (figure 3). Keep the side of the tines facing the audience to hide the bent tine.

5. Use your left index finger to rub the space between the straight and bent tines of the fork. Do it slowly for about seven seconds, then s-l-o-w-l-y turn the fork so it faces your audience as you continue stroking as shown at left. Your viewers will swear you're making the tines part!

The Magnetic Knife

Looking for some entertainment at dinnertime? Here's how to cast a spell that magically magnetizes a knife so it sticks to your hand. (At least your family will think so.) To really amaze an audience, do the same thing with your Never-Fail Magician's Wand (page 18).

WHAT YOU NEED

• a dull table knife (no sharp points, please)

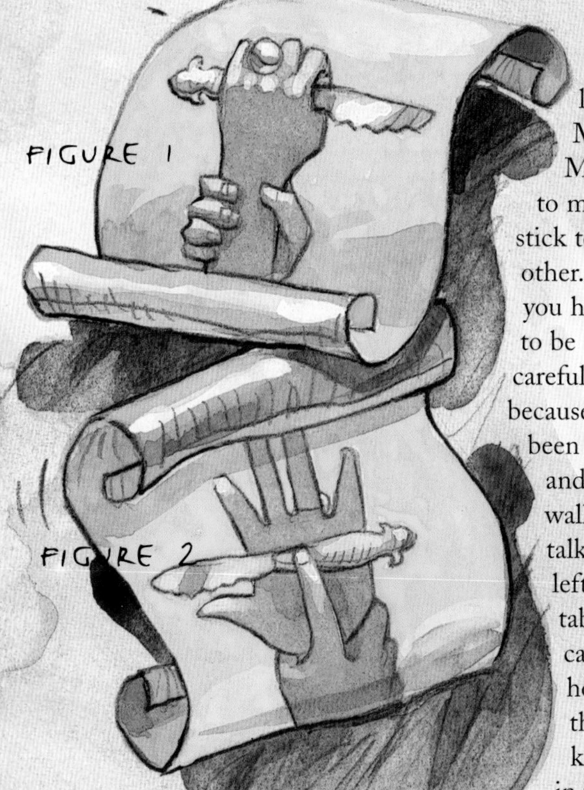

FIGURE 1

FIGURE 2

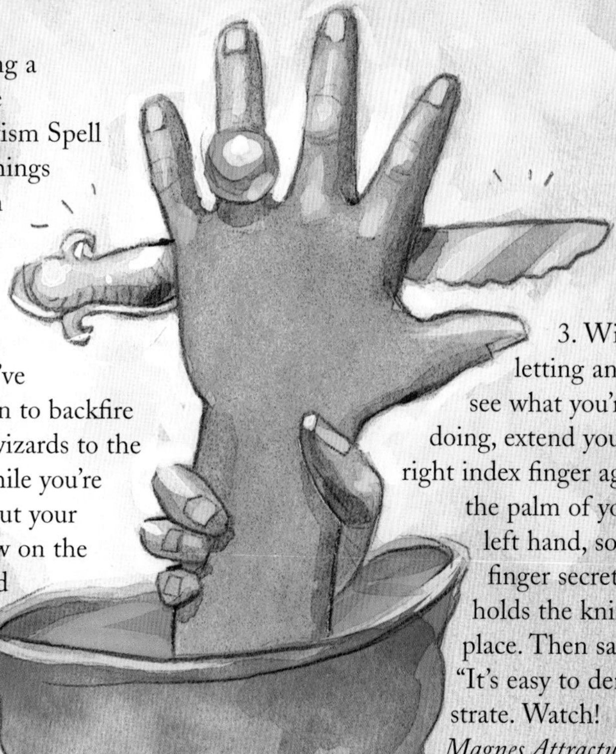

INSTRUCTIONS

1. Make sure you're seated far enough away from your audience that they have only a front view of you.

2. Pick up the knife from the table as you say, "You know, I've been learning a Mobile Magnetism Spell to make things stick to each other. But you have to be careful because they've been known to backfire and pin wizards to the wall!" While you're talking, put your left elbow on the table and casually hold the knife in your left hand with the back of your hand towards your audience. At the same time, use your right hand to grasp your left wrist (figure 1).

3. Without letting anyone see what you're doing, extend your right index finger against the palm of your left hand, so the finger secretly holds the knife in place. Then say, "It's easy to demonstrate. Watch! *Magnes Attractus!*" [mag-NESS uh-TRACK-tuss]

4. Spread the fingers of your left hand (figure 2) so it looks like you've let go of the knife. But there it is for anyone to see, the knife is still "magnetized" to your left hand.

107

Floating Banquet Ware,

or the Perpetual Motion Plate

Well, okay, technically a plate doesn't entirely float in this illusion, but it's amazing nonetheless. After balancing a dinner plate and forks on the end of a needle, you'll send everything spinning. I do NOT recommend doing this trick with your mother's best china, however, unless you're highly proficient in casting an Unbreakable Breakables Spell.

WHAT YOU NEED

- helpful adult wizard
- sharp knife
- 2 corks (the size found in a wine bottle)
- 4 table forks
- inexpensive ceramic dinner plate
- sandpaper
- clean bottle with a cork stopper
- water or sand
- thimble
- sewing needle

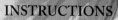

INSTRUCTIONS

1. Have an adult wizard use the knife to slice the corks in half lengthwise. Stick one fork in each cork half so it forms slightly less than a 90° angle relative to the cork.

2. Use the sandpaper to slightly roughen the center of the bottom of the plate.

3. Fill the bottle with water or sand, and cork it. Have the adult wizard put on the thimble and thrust the head of the needle (not the pointed end) straight down into the cork, leaving a portion exposed above the cork.

4. Holding the plate at the horizontal, position the fork and cork assemblies at equal distances around the top of the plate. The flat side of each cork should rest on top of the plate, and part of the exposed fork tines should rest solidly against the plate rim so they don't wobble. The fork handles should angle under the plate and point towards the bottle.

5. Center the plate assembly over the needle and gently, slowly set it down, balancing it on the point of the needle. Give the edge of the plate a push to start it spinning. You and your audience will be amazed by how long it spins.

The Levitated Salt Shaker

Because salt was so precious and important back in the days before refrigeration, it was thought to possess powerful good magic. When someone asks you to pass the salt at the dinner table, here's how to extend your hand, merely touch your fingertips to the top of the salt shaker, and slowly raise it from the table. Or so it seems. When a wizard is around (that means you) people learn to expect the unexpected.

WHAT YOU NEED

- ring
- toothpick
- salt shaker with perforations of a size able to grasp an inserted toothpick

INSTRUCTIONS

1. Put the ring on a finger of your dominant hand, and hide the toothpick in a pocket.

2. While you're sitting at the table, secretly position the toothpick so one end is secured under the ring, the toothpick runs between two adjoining fingers, and a small portion of the other end of the toothpick protrudes past your fingertips.

3. When someone asks for the salt, reach for it with your wrist cocked and fingers pointing straight down. Insert the toothpick into a hole in the salt shaker. Maintaining the pressure of your fingers on the toothpick, raise the shaker.

4. To release the shaker from its "spell" after you've set it down on the table, continue to hold the toothpick firmly with your fingers. Immediately reach over with your left hand, detach the shaker, and offer it to your astonished dinner partner. In the meantime, quickly remove your right hand and hide the toothpick in your pocket.

Wizard Post (AS THE BRITISH CALL IT)

Imagine going to the mailbox, picking up your mail, and finding a mysterious envelope. Imagine opening the card inside . . . and a grand racket startles you! You can make this card to send to a friend or to hand to a member of your audience. Stand back after you do so!

WHAT YOU NEED

• 1 blank or printed greeting card and envelope

• magical patterns and decorating materials on page 138 and 141 (optional)

• 1 length of wire , 6 inches (15.2 cm) long*

• wire cutter

• round-nosed pliers

• 2 short rubber bands (orthodontic bands are perfect)

• scissors

• 1 x 2-inch (2.5 x 5 cm) length of construction or heavy paper

• white craft glue

• split key ring

*Use a length of wire cut from a wire coat hanger or galvanized wire.

INSTRUCTIONS

1. Decorate the card as desired. If you'll use it as part of your performance, address the envelope to a member of the audience and write in a return address such as, Professor Marvel's Correspondence School of the Mystical Arts.

2. Use the pliers to make small hooks at each end of the wire. Bend the wire into a U shape (figure 1).

3. Slip one end of a rubber band around the split ring. Loop the other end back through the opposite loop. This secures the band to the ring (figure 2). Repeat with a second rubber band.

4. Use the scissors to cut the length of construction paper in half lengthwise.

5. Lay the U-shape wire inside the card. Put a small amount of glue on each end of the paper strips. Glue them to the card while holding down the wire (figure 3). Let the glue dry completely.

6. Before you slip the card into the envelope, twist the split key ring, at the same time twisting the rubber bands tightly. Keeping the twist in the rubber bands, fold the card and slip it into the envelope.

7. Now hand the envelope to an unsuspecting audience member and ask her to open it. RAT-A-TAT-TAT! The envelope will suddenly vibrate and make a loud, clattering noise. Hopefully, your audience member has a good sense of humor!

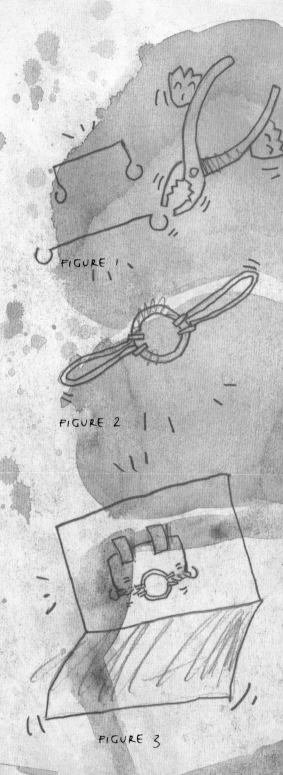

FIGURE 1

FIGURE 2

FIGURE 3

Magical Union of the *Flying Paper Clips*

Sometimes the best magic is created with everyday items, especially objects donated by your audience. A paper clip and paper money is about as ordinary as it gets. Therefore you'll amaze your friends all the more with this deceptively simple trick. Practice until you can slip the clips onto the bill exactly as shown below, so your motions appear totally effortless and the effect is truly magical!

WHAT YOU NEED

- 2 metal paper clips
- paper money, any denomination
- Never-Fail Magic Wand (page 18)

INSTRUCTIONS

1. Show your audience the two paper clips, passing them around for inspection. Announce that, with the help of a volunteer, you are going to magically join the two paper clips without touching them.

2. Ask for someone to donate a hundred dollar bill. If one does not appear, keep asking for a bill in a smaller denomination (50, 20, 10, 5, 1?) until someone volunteers one.

3. Make a big show of smoothing out the bill. Then fold it, as shown above.

4. Slip the clips onto the bill, as shown. Pronounce some magic phrases such as, *E Pluribus Unum!* or *Novus Ordo Seclorum!* [EE PLUR-IH-buss OOO-num or KNOW-vuss OR-dough suh-KLOR-um] and wave your wand over the bill.

5. Ask for a volunteer. (I recommend you ask the donor of the money.)

6. Have the volunteer grasp both ends of the bill. As you wave your wand over the bill, ask the volunteer to quickly and sharply pull both ends of the bill at the same time. The paper clips will go flying in the air. *Alakazaam!* They're magically joined.

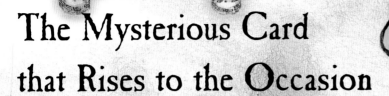

The Mysterious Card that Rises to the Occasion

The American magician Howard Thurston was famed for making playing cards float above a deck on command. I also remember him fondly for his kindness to young people who wanted to become magicians. So in Howard's honor, here's how to confound your audience with your magical powers of persuasion by making a playing card rise.

WHAT YOU NEED

- tall drinking glass with tapered sides*
- acrylic paints in four different colors
- small brush
- bar of soap
- playing cards

*Only a drinking glass with tapered sides will do. Accept no substitutes! If you don't have one handy in your cupboard, then go to a second-hand store and buy one that has the correct shape.

113

FIGURE 1

FIGURE 2

INSTRUCTIONS

1. Wash and dry the glass. Paint $^1/_2$-inch-wide (1.3 cm) stripes of the same color on the outside of the glass, on opposite sides (figure 1). Paint two stripes of each color and let dry. You'll have eight stripes in all. Don't use the painted glass to drink from; reserve it just for this trick.

2. Before your performance, rub the bar of soap on the inside of the glass along two opposing stripes of the same color. Make the soap stripes as wide as the painted stripes (figure 2). Remember which stripes you've marked with the soap, or your powers of persuasion won't work!

The Illusion

Making the Cards Rise

1. Show the empty glass to the audience and select someone to inspect the deck of cards. When she's satisfied that the deck isn't rigged, you can proceed. Ask someone else to shuffle the cards several times. Then ask a third person to select any card from the deck and to hand the card to you (figure 3).

2. This is where you need to remember which stripes you marked with soap! Push the card down into the glass, aligning it with any unsoaped pair of stripes. Ask someone to command the card to rise. It won't budge, of course. Remove the card from the glass and insert it into the deck.

3. Ask someone else to pick a card, and repeat step 2.

4. Ask one last person to select a card from the deck, but this time have them hand it to you. Slip the card into the glass along the soaped stripes. Utter a magical command, "*Sapindas floten!*" [suh-PIN-duss FLOW-tun], and wave your free hand over the glass. The card will slowly rise (figure 4).

Sapindas floten

FIGURE 3

FIGURE 4

115

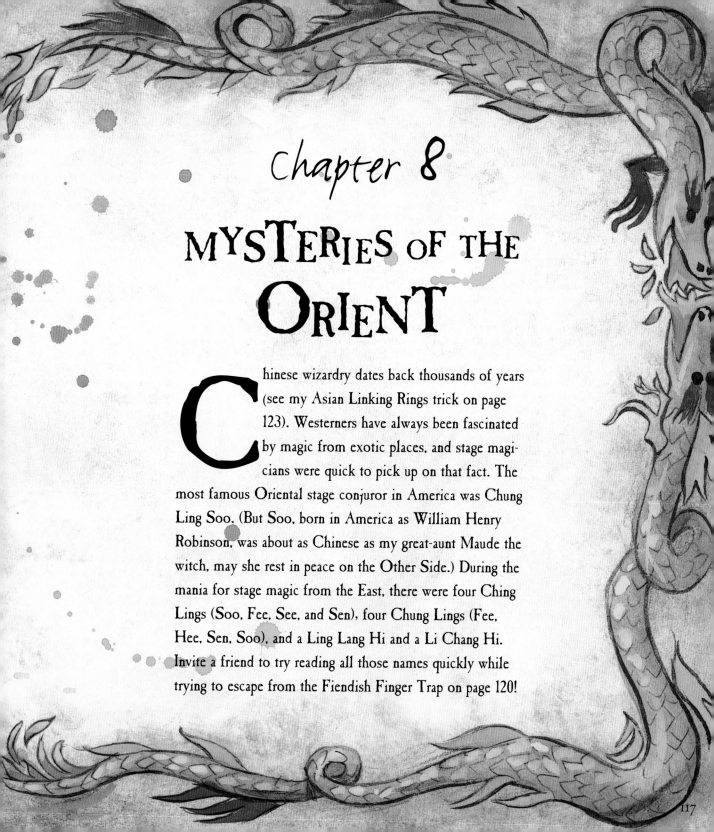

Chapter 8

MYSTERIES OF THE ORIENT

Chinese wizardry dates back thousands of years (see my Asian Linking Rings trick on page 123). Westerners have always been fascinated by magic from exotic places, and stage magicians were quick to pick up on that fact. The most famous Oriental stage conjuror in America was Chung Ling Soo. (But Soo, born in America as William Henry Robinson, was about as Chinese as my great-aunt Maude the witch, may she rest in peace on the Other Side.) During the mania for stage magic from the East, there were four Ching Lings (Soo, Fee, See, and Sen), four Chung Lings (Fee, Hee, Sen, Soo), and a Ling Lang Hi and a Li Chang Hi. Invite a friend to try reading all those names quickly while trying to escape from the Fiendish Finger Trap on page 120!

Lady Tze's
Magical Chinese Pagoda

I named this magical production in honor of the Chinese spirit
Lady Tze, who has been helping female *wu* (wizards) for centuries.
She gives her favorites special literary talent, plus skill at foretelling the
future. With practice, you can make a pagoda so deftly on stage your
audience will be quite impressed. But be careful! This production is for
older wizards and sorceresses who can handle a sharp knife safely.

PROCEED
WITH
CAUTION!

WHAT YOU NEED

• long, narrow strip of paper (its
dimensions may vary), or multiple,
same-size strips in contrasting colors
• 1 small wooden dowel or stick,
longer than the width of the paper
• sharp knife

FIGURE 1

FIGURE 2

FIGURE 3

FIGURE 4

INSTRUCTIONS

1. If desired, start with several colors of paper stacked on top of each other, or start with a single strip of paper. Fold the end of the paper over several times (figure 1), then roll up the paper around the stick (figure 2).

2. Remove the stick from the rolled-up paper, then use the dull edge of the knife to crease the edges of the roll to flatten it.

3. Use the knife to make two cuts in the middle of the roll (figure 3), cutting deep enough to reach to the folds you first made at the end of the strip of paper in step 1.

4. Now cut through the folds of paper that are between the cuts. Bend the ends to form the U shape, as shown in figure 4.

5. Gently insert the tip of the knife under the first fold and pull it out gently, coaxing the paper to expand until you have a full-fledged pagoda.

The Indian Rope Trick, the Indian Basket Trick, and Other Mysterious Feats of Fakirs and Far Eastern Sages

I saw one of most amazing—and stomach-churning—magic tricks ever during a trip across Africa and the Orient with explorer Ibn Batuta. (He didn't know he was travelling with me—I was disguised as a carpet at the time. But that's a different story.) A local kahn (king, in India) invited Batuta to a feast and magic show. Batuta's host promised the most famous *indrajal* (magic) of them all: the Indian Rope Trick.

A fakir hurled a ball with a long rope attached to it high into the sky. The ball disappeared from view, but the rope's end trailed on the ground. His apprentice climbed the rope, hand over hand, until he, too, disappeared. The fakir demanded he come down. No response. So the fakir tightened his turban, put a knife between his teeth, and climbed the rope. Suddenly legs, fingers, and other blood-stained bits of the apprentice rained down on the dinner guests. (Being a rug at the time, it's a good thing I didn't have a stomach.) As people screamed and ran—one sheik even passed out cold—the fakir descended. He collected the pieces and reassembled his apprentice, who then stood up, smiled, and bowed! Incredible. Funny, though, no one wanted dessert.

I've never approved of casual dismemberment of one's apprentices, however, so no matter how much you beg, I'm not sharing the fakir's secrets. But allow me to describe the Indian Basket Trick. An assistant climbs into a basket. Without warning, the magician plunges a sharp sword into it, again and again. As blood leaks out, people of course scream and turn to run. But there's the assistant behind them, completely unharmed! (Do NOT, under any circumstance, put a friend or your younger brother in a basket and stick it with sharp objects!)

Once, I was in China learning the art of thunder writing. (It's a sure way to get rid of goblins, and one had been pestering me for 82 years.) I sat in on a performance of the Water Bowl Trick by my friend Pei Ling Zhao. (Chinese magicians always had an obsession with fishbowls. Maybe it's because they think fish bring luck.) She walked onstage with a huge cauldron of water strapped to the small of her back, so the audience couldn't see it. As she stepped aside, the cauldron "appeared" on stage. One night, to liven things up, I slipped a Chinese river piranha into the cauldron. After Pei Ling set the cauldron down, the piranha leapt up, teeth snapping. (The look on her face made me wish the camera had been invented.) But, like all great magicians, Pei Ling just took it in stride, and the audience never suspected what the real trick was.

Fiendish Finger Trap

The origins of this clever device are as mysterious as the Orient itself. Legend has it that Mee See Lots, the apprentice of famed Chinese sorcerer Wei Too Long, was too lazy to learn complex Entrapment Spells, so he invented this substitute. You'll enjoy your friend's puzzled look when you ask him to insert a finger in each end. I suggest making several traps at one time. You'll want to have more than one on hand, so to speak!

WHAT YOU NEED

- colored construction paper
- ruler
- pencil
- scissors
- 1 dowel, 1/2 inch (1.3 cm) in diameter, 6 inches (15.2 cm) long or longer
- white craft glue
- masking tape or rubber bands

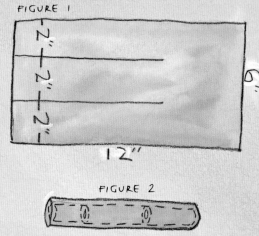

FIGURE 1

2"
2"
2"

12"

FIGURE 2

INSTRUCTIONS

1. Measure and draw 6 x 12-inch (15.2 x 30.5 cm) rectangles on your construction papers.

2. Cut out the rectangles.

3. Mark two evenly spaced lines running parallel to the long edge of each rectangle. Make each line about 8 inches (20.3 cm) long (figure 1).

4. Cut along each of the two lines.

5. Place the dowel on the cut end of a rectangle. Roll the rectangle tightly onto the dowel (figure 2). Put a line of the glue along the edge of the rectangle and glue it together to form a tube. Use small bits of the tape or rubber bands to hold the tube closed until the glue dries.

6. When the glue is dry, slip the dowel from the tube. Using the other rectangles, repeat steps 1 through 5 to make as many tubes as desired.

7. Now ask a volunteer to place one forefinger in each end of the tube. Easy enough, right? Now invite him to try to remove his fingers. The coiled, cut ends inside the tube pull out and hold the fingers snugly.

HE'S TRAPPED!

The Mystery of the Miniature Tea Caddy

Thanks to their trade with the Chinese, the British became a nation of tea drinkers. Tea was so valuable that it was stored in locked tea caddies. The very first trick the English boy wizard—oops, I mean young stage magician—John Nevil Maskelyne created was a magic tea caddy. He placed a ring inside, bound the tea caddy with tape, and handed it to a spectator. When the box was opened, it was empty, and the ring was on Maskelyne's finger! Here's how to create your own, smaller version of a tea caddy that makes things vanish.

WHAT YOU NEED

- small, round, commercially made papier-mâché box*
- acrylic paints
- small brush
- poster board in a color matching one of the paints
- pencil
- scissors
- gel pens and puff paint (optional)

*You can find these brown boxes in different sizes at craft stores.

INSTRUCTIONS

1. Paint the inside of your box to match the poster board. Let the paint dry.

FIGURE 1

2. Trace around the bottom of your box onto the poster board. Use the scissors to cut out the circle. Fit the circle into the bottom of the box, trimming it as needed so it moves slightly (figure 1).

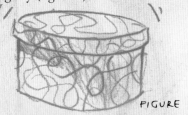

FIGURE 2

3. Paint the exteriors of the lid and bottom part of the box. Let dry, then use the gel pens or puff paint to add fancy designs, dots, or squiggles. It's important that the designs on the top and bottom of the box look the same. A decorated box helps distract the attention of the audience (figure 2). Let dry.

The Illusion

Using the Caddy to Make a Coin Disappear

1. Slip the poster board circle into the bottom of the box while you're offstage.

2. Open the box and tilt the top and bottom so the audience can peer inside the box. Be careful not to dislodge the poster board circle.

3. Ask for a coin from the audience. Place it in the bottom part of the box.

4. Put the lid on the box. Shake the box so the audience can hear the coin rattling. Pronounce a magic phrase, and at the same time, turn over the box so the cardboard circle inside covers the coin.

5. Separate the box once again, and tilt the top and bottom just enough so the audience can peer inside (but the coin and circle won't come tumbling out!).

6. Reverse steps 4 and 5. *Voilà!* Show the audience the coin that has magically reappeared.

Asian Linking Rings

I first saw this trick performed several centuries ago at a two-day banquet given by the Vietnamese sorcerer Mee Too Phat. I tried to be polite and eat everything I was offered, but after dozens of courses I had to perform a Hollow Leg Charm on myself to keep up. Anyway, here's how to use cut paper rings to astonish your audience.

WHAT YOU NEED

- ruler
- pencil
- scissors
- several sheets of newspaper
- gold acrylic paint (optional)
- paintbrush (optional)
- glue

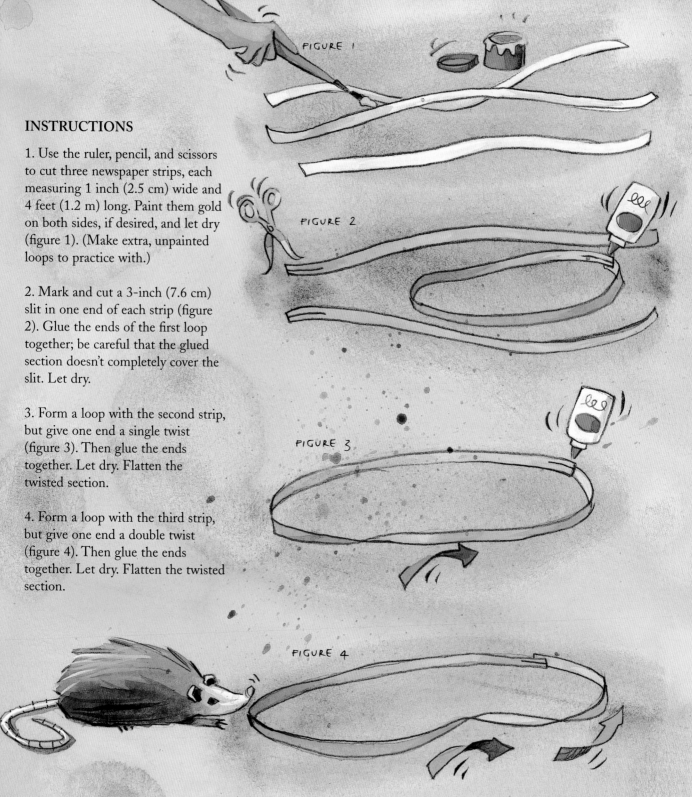

INSTRUCTIONS

1. Use the ruler, pencil, and scissors to cut three newspaper strips, each measuring 1 inch (2.5 cm) wide and 4 feet (1.2 m) long. Paint them gold on both sides, if desired, and let dry (figure 1). (Make extra, unpainted loops to practice with.)

2. Mark and cut a 3-inch (7.6 cm) slit in one end of each strip (figure 2). Glue the ends of the first loop together; be careful that the glued section doesn't completely cover the slit. Let dry.

3. Form a loop with the second strip, but give one end a single twist (figure 3). Then glue the ends together. Let dry. Flatten the twisted section.

4. Form a loop with the third strip, but give one end a double twist (figure 4). Then glue the ends together. Let dry. Flatten the twisted section.

FIGURE 1

FIGURE 2

FIGURE 3

FIGURE 4

The Illusion

Linking the Three Loops

1. To prepare for your performance, lay the scissors and three loops (with twisted sides down and their joins where you can grab them) on a table.

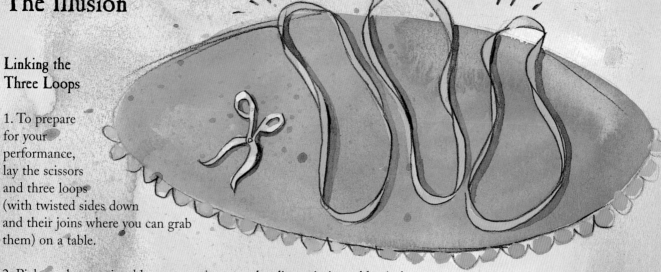

2. Pick up the untwisted loop at a point near the slit cut in it, and begin by telling your audience about Mee Too Phat's two-day banquet. While using the scissors to cut the loop at the slit and down the middle (figure 5), continue your story by saying, "Phat's conjuror taught me the secret of an amazing feat. First, I'll cut one loop into two. Anyone can do that, right?" Display the two loops (figure 6) and let them drop to the table.

3. Pick up the loop with the double twist. Start cutting at the slit and say, "But now I'll use a magic spell. *Circulus Rotundus!* {SIR-kew-luss row-TUN-duss]" As you finish cutting, announce, "Aha! The two loops are linked!" Show your audience, then drop the loops onto the table.

FIGURE 5   FIGURE 6

4. Pick up the last loop with the single twist. Hiding the twist, start cutting and say, "So what happens if we try to do this backwards? *Rotundus Reversus Double Plus!*" You've now produced a single, giant loop.

Chapter 9

YOU ARE FEELING S-L-E-E-E-P-Y

MIND READING & OTHER FEATS OF MENTAL MAGIC

People have always been fascinated by a wizard's ability to see into the future as well as other people's thoughts, which is why stage illusions involving mind reading are so powerful. It takes only a simple deck of cards to stupefy people with the Abracadabra Card Mystery on page 129. Or use your mental powers to magically alter an image before their very eyes with the Mystery of the Magic Photograph on page 134. But take this prophecy business with a grain of salt! Consider Simon Forman, a very successful astrologer back in merry old England. Legend says he predicted the exact day and time of his own demise. But if that was so, why would he be rowing a boat in the middle of the River Thames at the exact moment he expired? (Because that's what happened.)

Amazing ^ Amulet

ABRACADABRA

For centuries, people have used the Abracadabra charm to cure illness and ward off bad luck. You can direct the power of Abracadabra! depending on which way the triangle is aimed. For disappearing-type magic, wear the amulet so the letters dwindle down to a point. Wear it the other way to encourage growth. Either way, it helps you remember how to spell the word!

WHAT YOU NEED

- empty ball-point pen
- 1 disposable aluminum oven liner or pie plate
- scissors
- hole punch
- 1 magazine
- 1 thin ribbon, 24 inches (61 cm) long

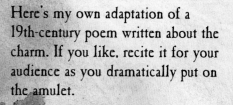

Here's my own adaptation of a 19th-century poem written about the charm. If you like, recite it for your audience as you dramatically put on the amulet.

Each under each in even order place,
But the last letter in each line efface.
As by degrees the elements grow few
Still take away, but fix the residue,
Till at last, one letter stands alone
And the whole dwindles to a tapering cone.
Tie about the neck with a flaxen string
Might the good 'twill to the magic bring,
Its wondrous potency shall my powers aid, Wizards helped by forces best unsaid.

INSTRUCTIONS

1. Study the illustration, then use the pen to outline a triangle on the aluminum to the size you wish. Cut it out.

2. Punch a hole at the top point or base of the triangle, or both, so you can redirect its powers at will.

3. Place a scrap piece of aluminum on the magazine. Practice using the ball-point pen to copy the lettering on the metal. Press the pen on the metal to engrave the letters. Or concentrate really hard and write backwards. Then, when you turn the aluminum, the surface will reveal embossed letters.

4. Lay the triangle on the magazine and copy the word "ABRA-CADABRA" onto the metal.

5. Thread the ribbon through the hole, and tie the amulet around your neck. Wear it in good magic!

Abracadabra Card Mystery

Correctly spelling difficult words is an important skill for a wizard to learn, but it's also a crucial part of performing this trick successfully. Speak the letters to yourself as you practice: A-b-r-a-c-a-d-a-b-r-a! You'll be amazed by the results.

WHAT YOU NEED

• deck of playing cards (minus the jokers)

INSTRUCTIONS

1. Ask for a volunteer to shuffle the deck of playing cards two or three times. Then have her deal you a stack of 21 cards from the deck.

2. Pick up the cards. Deal three cards from left to right. Return to your left side and deal six additional rows in the same way. Arrange the three columns of seven cards each so you can see the markings on all cards (figure 1).

3. Ask your volunteer to silently select any card in one of the columns. Have the volunteer point to the column which contains the chosen card (but not the card itself).

4. Pick up one of the other columns, the chosen column, and then the remaining column.

5. Deal the cards out as you did in step 2. Have your volunteer point to the column which contains the chosen card (again, without disclosing her choice).

6. Pick up one of the other columns, the chosen column, and the remaining column.

7. Repeat steps 2 through 4 once more. Now it's time to magically locate the chosen card.

8. Hold the cards face down in your hand as if you're going to deal them out again. Ask your volunteer, "Do you know the meaning of the magic word Abracadabra? It means, 'Find what I seek!'"

9. Deal the cards face up from the stack of cards, spelling the word "a-b-r-a-c-a-d-a-b-r-a" out loud letter by letter as you deal, one letter per card. As you pronounce the last (a) of Abracadabra, the card your volunteer secretly chose magically reveals itself!

The Persistence of Memory

I used to visit my writer friend Marcel whenever I was in Paris, and every time I did, he asked me to perform this illusion. He said he found it inspirational. Marcel was a shut-in, you see, and the numbers that are part of this trick glowed quite nicely in the darkness of his bedroom, where the cork-lined walls and all his piles of paper absorbed all the light. When you perform this piece of magic, your friends will be amazed by your mind-reading ability. Why? Because you will announce the digit that a volunteer secretly selected.

WHAT YOU NEED

- ruler
- luminous tape*
- scissors
- 4 x 4-inch (10.2 x 10.2 cm) square of poster board
- fine line marking pen
- scrap of poster board
- calculator
- pencil
- paper
- square of dark cloth, large enough to cover your head and face

*Home improvement and craft stores sell glow-in-the-dark tape. Reflective tape (like the kind you put on your bicycle) won't work.

130

The Illusion

Mind Reading a Selected Number

INSTRUCTIONS

1. Measure and cut three 3-$\frac{1}{2}$-inch-long (8.9 cm) strips of luminous tape.

2. Attach the strips to the square of poster board.

3. Use the fine line marking pen to outline four squares of identical size on each tape strip. Number the squares with any numbers you desire (figure 1).

4. Cut out a small square from the scrap piece of poster board. Make it the same size as one of the squares you drew on a tape strip.

1. Perform this trick in a brightly lit area. The area under an illuminated lamp on a tabletop is a perfect place. Place the numbered square, small square, calculator, pencil, and paper on the table.

2. Cover your head and face with the dark cloth. Turn your back to the audience, and ask a volunteer to come to the table and select a number on the square. Tell him to show the number to the audience, before covering the number with the small square.

3. Now you need to keep talking to give the "magic" time to work. Ask the volunteer to silently perform the following sequence of math operations on the calculator. Announce, "These operations, plus the ancient phenomenon magicians call persistence of memory, will enable me to identify the number chosen earlier by my volunteer." Give the volunteer lots of directions of things to do (which really have nothing to do with the trick, but do buy you some time). For example, say to the volunteer, "Add

the year of your birth and 200. Divide this number by 20. Multiply the answer by 3. Subtract your age from this number. Now divide the number by 10. Add 42 to the answer. Write the answer down on the piece of paper, fold it up, and give it to an audience member."

With your back still turned, ask the volunteer to remove the square of poster board that covered the chosen number. Then say, "Will you please concentrate your mental emanations towards me. It will help me detect the thoughts you had a few minutes ago."

5. Turn around, lift the dark cloth, and pick up the numbered card. Place the card in front of your face and cover your head again. Explain that the dark cloth allows you to concentrate.

6. The tape will of course glow in the darkness under the cloth, and the number that was covered will not be as bright as the others. Pretend to concentrate. Now tell your astounded audience which number was covered!

Messages from the Ether, or the
Magical Naming of Cards

One of the best conjurors with cards I ever knew was Girolamo Scotto, an Italian knight in the 1500s. He was quite a dandy and always wore a plumed hat. (The ladies were wild for him.) Whether Giro had a person mentally pick a card from a deck or a word from the pages inside a closed book, he always knew their secret! For this trick, you need a trustworthy helper with a decent memory. Time after time (that's a hint how this trick works) you'll be able to name the playing card a spectator chose while you were out of the room.

WHAT YOU NEED

- helpful wizard's assistant
- deck of playing cards
- pencil
- small slips of paper
- flat tabletop

INSTRUCTIONS

1. To prepare for this feat, you and your assistant must memorize figure 1, which depicts an imaginary clock face on a tabletop. The table is also divided into four quadrants, which represent the suits in a deck of cards: spades, diamonds, clubs, and hearts. This imaginary layout is how you and your assistant will communicate with each other. Read on.

2. To begin your performance, announce that you will demonstrate how easy it is for wizards to read people's minds and to pluck their thoughts right out of the air. Say, "I will now leave the room while one of you chooses a card from this deck. Please write the suit and number of the card on a slip of paper, and hand the pencil and paper to my assistant. And just so everyone knows which card was chosen, please silently display the card to the audience."

3. With that, leave the room. After the volunteer writes down her selection and displays the card to everyone, she should fold the slip of paper and hand it and the pencil to your assistant. Your assistant will then casually lay the paper in the quadrant of the table that matches the card's suit, the pencil pointing to the card's number.

4. When you return to the room, casually take note of the positioning of the paper and pencil. Then pick up the piece of paper and without opening the paper, announce the card's suit and number.

YOU'RE A GENIUS!

The Mystery of the Magic Photograph

The Bangs, a pair of psychic sisters in Chicago in the early 1900s, created "Spirit Paintings" onstage. Two large, blank canvases on easels were set on the stage. While an audience watched the sisters concentrate their mental powers, colorful paintings appeared, like magic, on their surfaces. Here's an updated version, which combines modern photography with your own mental powers. More than any other illusion in this book, this piece of magic requires ahead-of-time planning and crafting, but the effect is well worth the effort.

WHAT YOU NEED

- robe, hat, or any other clothing you'll wear when you perform this trick
- 8 x 10 inch (20.3 x 25.4 cm) picture frame, glass removed
- camera
- helpful adult wizard
- 8 x 10-inch (20.3 x 25.4 cm) school photo of yourself
- Now You See It, Now You Don't double-walled bag on page 28
- marking pen
- sheet of poster board or thin cardboard
- scissors
- glue stick
- stack of heavy books
- newspaper

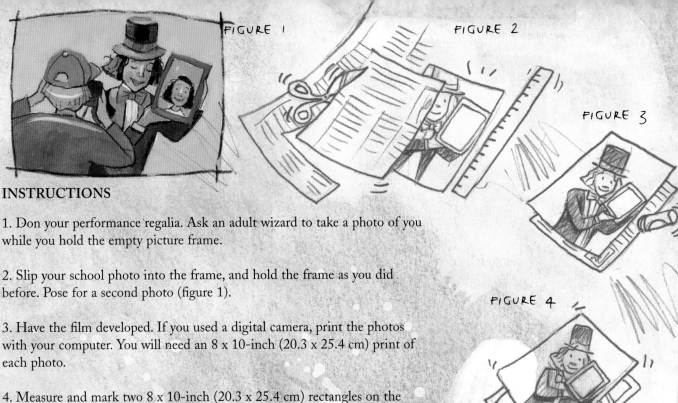

FIGURE 1

FIGURE 2

FIGURE 3

INSTRUCTIONS

1. Don your performance regalia. Ask an adult wizard to take a photo of you while you hold the empty picture frame.

2. Slip your school photo into the frame, and hold the frame as you did before. Pose for a second photo (figure 1).

3. Have the film developed. If you used a digital camera, print the photos with your computer. You will need an 8 x 10-inch (20.3 x 25.4 cm) print of each photo.

4. Measure and mark two 8 x 10-inch (20.3 x 25.4 cm) rectangles on the poster board (figure 2). Cut them out.

5. Use the glue stick to mount the photos on the poster board, one per rectangle (figure 3). Set a couple of heavy books on top of each one, and let dry.

6. On the photo that shows you wearing your performance costume and holding your framed school picture, write the date of your show or autograph the photo with your name and, "Best wishes from a truly spectacular magician!"

7. Lay the photo that shows you holding the empty frame face up on a sheet of newspaper. Trace around the outline of the photo (figure 4). Cut out the shape on the newspaper and glue it to the back of the photo. Lay a heavy book on top, and let it dry.

8. Insert the photo with your school picture inside the frame.

9. The photo (of you holding the empty frame) will be placed on top of the photo you put inside the frame. Carefully trim the edges to fit just inside the frame edge.

10. Make a double-walled bag, as described on page 28 (figure 6).

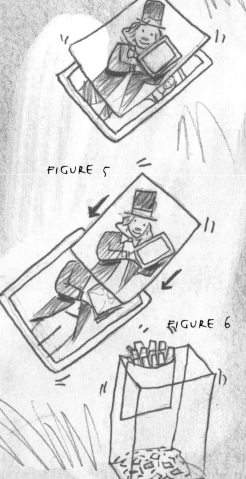

FIGURE 4

FIGURE 5

FIGURE 6

The Illusion

Making a Photograph Magically Appear

In addition to the photo props you made, you'll need the following items to perform the trick.

- **50 or more 2 x 3-inch (5 x 7.6 cm) strips of paper**
- **pencils**
- **newspaper**
- **soup bowl**

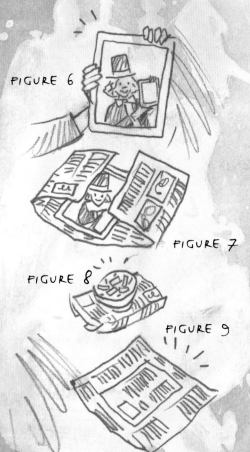

FIGURE 6

FIGURE 7

FIGURE 8

FIGURE 9

1. Before the performance, write your name on several of the strips of paper. Place these strips in the double-walled bag (the main part of the bag, not the secret pocket. Fold the bag flat.

2. On your magic table, place the double-walled bag, a sheet of newspaper, bowl, pencils, strips of paper, and the framed photo so it's flat and face up.

3. Now you're ready to perform. Pass out the blank strips of paper and pencils. Have each person in the room (including yourself) write down the name of someone in the room.

4. Pass the soup bowl so everyone can put their slip in it.

5. Carefully pick up the framed photo. Tilt the frame back ever so slightly to prevent the photo from falling out. Placing your fingertips at the top and side edges of the photo will help (figure 6). Tell the audience that you will now make a picture of someone in the room magically appear in the empty frame you've just shown them.

6. Spread a piece of newspaper on the table. Using your fingertips to carefully hold the picture in place, lay the frame face down on the table. Pick up the newspaper and cover the frame. Wrap the newspaper around the frame (figure 7), folding the sides first, then the top and bottom ends. Place the bowl of slips on top to hold the folds in place (figure 8).

7. Pick up the bag and open it. Use your fingers to open up the secret pocket. Pour the slips from the bowl into the secret pocket.

8. Holding the top of the bag closed, make a show of shaking up the slips of paper.

9. Open the bag, keeping your fingers over the opening of the secret pocket. Ask a volunteer from the audience to close their eyes and select a slip from the bag.

10. Ask the volunteer to read the name aloud. As he does so, walk to the table and begin unwrapping the frame. Keep it flat on the table as you unwrap it. When you unwrap the frame, the front photo will fall on the newspaper. It will be camouflaged from the audience because the back is covered with newspaper (figure 9).

11. Raise the picture frame, and show the audience who's in the picture!

The Phantom Stallion, the Enchanted Camel, & John Adams and the Learned Pig

Is it easier to train a pig than to become a magician? My English friend William Frederick Pinchbeck claimed it was. (But don't let that discourage you.) The Learned Pig was the opening act of William's show when he toured North America. The pink porcine wonder could do arithmetic and spell out words by picking cards off the floor. Of course, William had a few problems with his piggy costar demanding this and that; the food bills were shocking!

John Adams—yes, the second president of the United States and elder statesman of the American Revolution—requested a performance from the Learned Pig. (I don't know what Mrs. Adams had to say about having a pig in the White House, but she was a very understanding woman.) Pinchbeck later announced that the President had applauded the act. But rumor has it that when questioned about affairs of state, the Learned Pig refused to answer. When pressed, he squealed and hid beneath a desk.

After Pinchbeck tired of touring, he sat down and wrote a tell-all book, explaining how he had trained the pig to answer questions. When the pig was two months old, he laid several cards on the floor in front of him. Each time the pig picked up a card, Pinchbeck gave him a slice of apple. He then taught the pig to pick up a card with a bent corner whenever he sniffed. (The public never noticed that the duo never performed when Pinchbeck had a cold.) The biggest challenge to Pinchbeck was doing the arithmetic in his head very quickly. (At the time, I urged William to say more about how smart pigs are, but he could be rather pigheaded.)

The famous magician Harry Blackstone had an entire, ahem, stable of magical illusions that involved animals. His most famous was the Phantom Stallion. Harry saddled up a large white horse and rode him onto the stage and into a canvas tent. Attendants then quickly stripped the canvas from the tent and revealed a bare frame—and no stallion! Sometimes Harry would be gone, too, and other times he'd be standing there with the saddle between his legs and a confused look on his face. Meanwhile, the horse was hidden behind a false back to the tent that matched the background of the stage.

One day, while touring through Iowa, Blackstone was offered a camel. (And what was a camel doing in Iowa? Well, let's just say Harry's act needed some spicing up, a little whiff of the exotic. And apparating a camel from Arabia wasn't easy, even for a wizard. But I admit nothing.) That very night, Harry announced that his Enchanted Camel would disappear onstage. He did the Phantom Stallion trick but substituted the camel. Everything worked perfectly until the audience began to applaud. The camel, being a fairly vain creature, knew the applause was for him. He stuck out his head from behind the false back of the tent to take his bow and ruined the illusion of his own disappearance! Blackstone went back to his Phantom Stallion trick and the Enchanted Camel was put out to pasture. Oh well, I meant well.

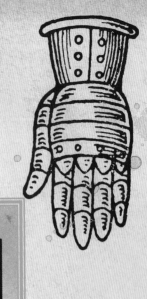

BASIC
DECORATING
INSTRUCTIONS

I've always enjoyed decorating my own
magical paraphernalia, and you will too.
Once you've chosen your magical patterns,
copy them freehand or use a photocopier to
copy, enlarge, or shrink them to the desired
size. There are many ways you can transfer
them to your chosen material.

To Decorate
FABRIC

Transfer patterns:

Photocopy the pattern. Cut it out and trace around it onto the fabric. Use a water-soluble marker, tailors' chalk, or a very sharp pencil.

Fabric paint:

Be sure to place newspaper under the fabric (or between two layers of fabric) before you use a paintbrush or stencil with fabric paint. Follow the manufacturer's instructions on the packaging for how to use an iron to heat-set the colors. Ask an adult wizard for help with this!

Cutouts:

Use the patterns to cut out shapes from contrasting colors and textures of fabric or craft foam. Attach the fabric shapes to the surface with white craft glue, hot glue, or fusible webbing.

Decorative attachments:

Add decorative trim, cording, or printed ribbon to the fabric, if desired. You can do this either by stitching the trim in place or by using fusible hem tape or fabric glue.

To Decorate
WOOD or PAPER

Transfer patterns:

Cut out photocopied patterns and trace around them with a pencil. You can tape them to vertical surfaces to keep them in place.

Acrylic paint:

Cover your work surface with newspaper or plastic sheeting. You can use any type of acrylic paint on wood. Spray paint provides a quick, even base coat if you're in a hurry. Just be sure to ask an adult wizard for help.

Other decorating materials:

Gel pens, puff paint, paint markers, glue, and colored pencils can be used on wood and paper. Let your wizardly imagination be your guide! Read the label to make sure the material is suitable for wood and/or paper.

BEND A METAL PIN INTO THESE SHAPES TO CREATE THE BOWL OF INVISIBLE FISH AND THE GHOSTLY GOBLET, ON PAGE 65

TEMPLATES

Get thee to a photocopier...

CUTTING TEMPLATES FOR THE MAGICAL CUTTING OF THE CARDS ON PAGE 64

YOU CAN TRACE OR COPY THESE IMAGES AND USE THEM TO DECORATE YOUR ROBE, POSTERS AND PROJECTS, OR DRAW YOU OWN.

FAREWELL from the Wizard

Now that you've read this book, I'm sure you're already thrilling and astonishing your friends and family with magical illusions and surprises of all kinds. I've enjoyed sharing my secrets and those of my magician friends with you. Use that knowledge well—and only for good.

As you make magic, I also hope you come to realize something that took me a couple of centuries to learn: how much fun and deeply satisfying it can be to give other people pleasure. Because one of a wizard's most important jobs, you know, is to keep awe and wonder alive in the world.

We may still have to tend to other matters, such as misbehaving dragons or the odd troll bashing about the countryside, but it's just as important for us to combat what I'll call the greyness of life. That's the ho-hum, seen-it-all, done-it-all attitude that some people adopt as they grow up. And to that I say, Nonsense! Wake up! Magic is all around us, if we just use our eyes to see it. And now you know lots of ways to make your own magic, too.

So I'll say goodbye for now. But I've always enjoyed using my Invisibility Spells and I like to watch young wizards as they progress in their magical skills. If you happen to hear a ghostly chuckle or feel the swish of an unseen cloak while you're practicing or performing, just keep going and enjoy yourself!

NOW, EXCUSE ME WHILE I DISAPPEAR

Index

continued

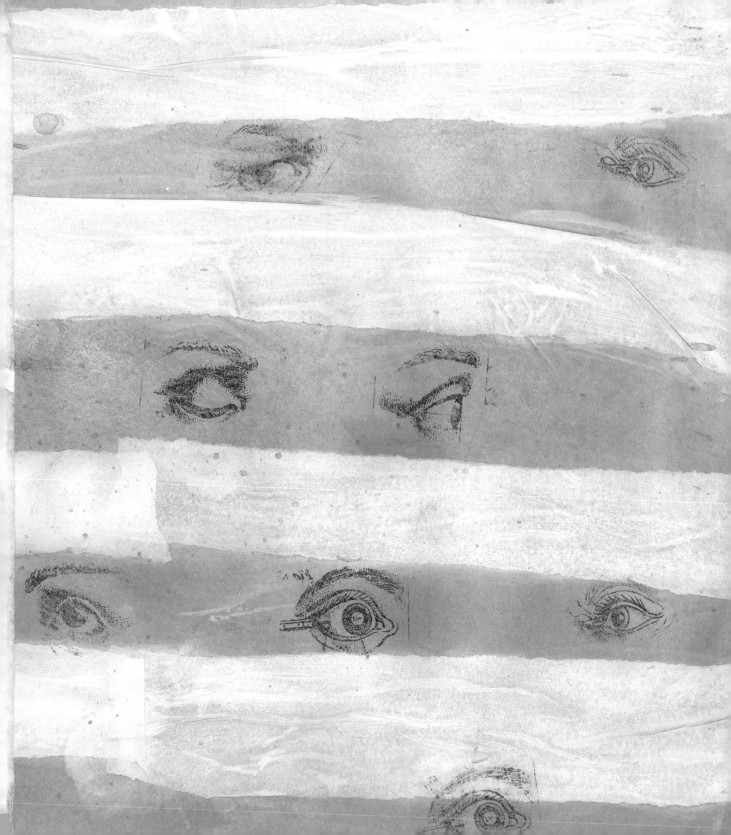